Accessing
the
Media

Accessing
the
Media

How to Get Good Press

JILL OSBORN

Skyhorse Publishing

Skyhorse Publishing books may be purchased in bulk at special discounts for sales promotion, corporate gifts, fund-raising, or educational purposes. Special editions can also be created to specifications. For details, contact the Special Sales Department, Skyhorse Publishing, 307 West 36th Street, 11th Floor, New York, NY 10018 or info@skyhorsepublishing.com.

Skyhorse® and Skyhorse Publishing® are registered trademarks of Skyhorse Publishing, Inc.®, a Delaware corporation.

Visit our website at www.skyhorsepublishing.com.

For more information about the author, visit Jill's website at https://JillOsborn.com.

10 9 8 7 6 5 4 3 2 1

Library of Congress Cataloging-in-Publication Data is available on file.

Cover design by Rain Saukas
Cover photo credit iStockphoto

Print ISBN: 978-1-5107-3025-0
Ebook ISBN: 978-1-5107-3026-7

Printed in the United States of America

For my resilient mom and brilliant writer,
Debra Hart Nelson. So the whole world knows
none of this would be possible if it wasn't for you.

Contents

Foreword

by Dr. Rob Peters

Working with the media may look different today than it did in generations past, but the tension in these relationships is nothing new.

Irishman Edmund Burke won the hearts of Americans for his support of the American Revolution. Years later, he, was asked to give the eulogy for Charles James Fox, the prominent British Whig statesman and the former British Foreign Minister. Both men had lived their lives in the public eye and had been brutalized by the press throughout their careers. There was a kinship there because of their commonalities with the media.

As the pastor of a large church, I often receive requests for quotes, comments, or a story from the media. Much like Edmund Burke, my first two decades of dealing with the press were filled with disappointment in how many of those interactions went. This frustration came to a head on November 23, 2007. The *Wall Street Journal* asked to interview me for an article about giving to religious charities. The interview covered a range of topics. My comments were supportive of the Christian discipline called "tithing." I was supportive of the concept of giving toward charitable organizations. Yet, when the article appeared that day in the *Journal,* the title given to the article was, "The Backlash against Tithing."

I was never given any indication the article was going to be written in a negative tone. Obviously, I learned a significant lesson that day, and I began to reconsider how I interacted with the press. I began to lay down ground rules when dealing with the media. For example, I now say, "If you don't use my entire quote, you are not free to use my quote at all." These are difficult lessons to learn, and even more difficult to practice in the moment of an interview.

We live in a day when leadership and communications are fraught with hazards. With social media providing access for everyone to be a reporter, a commentator, and an expert, the "fields are white unto harvest," with dangers and difficulty when it comes to communicating publicly on almost any topic. Every public figure needs to understand how to navigate these waters. Every person who has a message they are seeking to share needs to know how to engage the media.

In her book *Accessing the Media,* Jill Osborn describes how to engage the media and make the most of every opportunity. She explains how to get your message out through various media and keep it focused to avoid dilution. Detailing what to do before, during, and after the event, and providing a guide for leaders in how to engage and communicate with the press, Osborn masterfully describes what is required to get the most out of your time with the press. Having been on both sides of the microphone and camera, Osborn shares her expertise, experience, and insights with readers as they seek to stay on message and engage the media.

I commend this book to you, confident that you will become better equipped to navigate this challenging, yet necessary, dynamic.

Dr. Rob Peters is Senior Pastor of Calvary Baptist Church in Winston-Salem, North Carolina. He is the founder of Corpus, a ministry to revitalize America's churches. Dr. Peters is also author of the ReFocus process to assist churches in rediscovering their purpose. He has written three books, *Evangel-lies, Let's Chat,* and *The Dangerous Gift.* Dr. Peters speaks internationally to evangelical Christians through Calvary's Global Missions Initiative.

Acknowledgments

My sincere gratitude to my parents, Debra and Brett Nelson, for their support and for teaching me that anything was possible. Thank you to my husband, Justin, who is my rock. To my three angelic babies, Jaxson, Olliana, and Oaklee—you three are the best thing I will ever achieve. I'd like to sing praises to my sister, Mandy Haggerson, whose strength and wisdom I respect tremendously. To my brother, Nick, who shares my affinity for youthful games. To Nina and Susie, you all are full of strength. I love you all with every ounce of my heart.

Thank you to Rebecca Bugger, for her brilliance and insight. A special thank you to Joe Muster for taking this book to the next level. I'm so grateful to Phyllis Swanson for your love and expertise. To Dwight Sparks, who encouraged me to swing for the fences. Thank you to Dr. Rob Peters, Jeff Gravley, Aaron Berlin, Jim Williams, Congressman Richard Hudson, Mayor Pro Tem Michelle Barson, and Dan Mastro, for all the wisdom and words. Gretchen Carlson, our modern-day Susan B. Anthony—thank you for encouraging women like myself. Thank you to my editor, Joseph Craig, for his powerful editorial eye. Thank you to Dr. Gary Chapman for your time and counsel. Thank you to Cameron Kent for your friendship and instruction. Also, thank you to Gary W. Moore who helped me pave the way. I am indebted to Jim Lentz, and Tom and Barbara Mahannah, who have been there for my family. Thank you to John Morrow for your assistance. Thank you to Adam Shepherd and author Ashley Papa, who has been a sounding board in my professional and personal life. Thank you to my Oak Valley Housewives, my girlfriends in Clemmons, and especially Whitney Jellar, Sarah Oxford, Whitney Ewing, and Catherine Spross. For the morning pep talks and java, my gratitude to those at Starbucks in Clemmons, North Carolina. Thank you to Sean Dalton and Kimrey Rhinehardt, for your mentoring throughout the years. Thanks also to those not mentioned above. So many of you have impacted my life and my writing that I could go on saying for the rest of my life, "Thank you to . . ."

Finally, thank you to my fellow journalists who verify their sources, write honest reports, and sometimes risk their lives.

Chapter 1

Why You Need the Media

The media's the most powerful entity on earth. They have the power to make the innocent guilty and to make the guilty innocent, and that's power. Because they control the minds of the masses.

—Malcolm X

The media controls the world. What is read on the web, heard on the radio, or seen on television shapes the way people think. If you have a message that needs to be heard, you need to understand how the media works.

The press can get votes for politicians and put cash in the pockets of businesses and charities. It can also destroy the fortunes of powerful people overnight. So what is the key to receiving positive media? You will soon receive this inside knowledge by understanding the three points of contact with the press, which I will explain in detail. But, let's first examine why you must strategically and successfully cultivate an ally in the most powerful entity: the media.

Getting press is an effective way to get your branded message out to a broad range of people. It creates a buzz about your message, your product, or your charity of choice. The media entices other vendors, volunteers, and voters. People are impressed when they hear you on the radio, see you on TV, or read about you in the paper. The phenomenon of being impressed by those in the limelight dates back to our prehistoric society. We follow leaders who receive more attention than us. Most people cannot obtain news coverage. Therefore, those who do move up higher on the social hierarchy.

Daniel Kruger, an evolutionary psychologist from the University of Michigan, explains the psychology behind the fascination of those in the spotlight. He says that an individual believes it is important to follow the thought process of leaders for several purposes. "One is just learning what high-status individuals do so you might more effectively become one. And two, it's basically political. Knowing what is going on with high-status individuals, you'd be better able to navigate the social scene." Kruger goes on to say that celebrity obsession is created on purpose. Even talk show hosts are on social media trying to relate even more to their audience in order to connect with viewers. Kruger acknowledges, "It's savvy marketing."

Without question, the media has a powerful influence on the "minds of the masses," as Malcom X noted. As a result, countries around the world control the press by co-opting journalists, putting them in jail, and even executing them. Look at China. According to a story by the *New York Times*, foreign reporters were videotaped and followed so closely they could not conduct interviews. For Chinese reporters, it is even worse. Their freedom of speech is extremely limited. The Nieman Foundation for Journalism at Harvard observed the treatment of Chinese journalists. The report notes, "In some cases, those who run afoul of the government have been arrested and forced to confess to crimes on state-run television."

In Mexico, a journalist was gunned down and shot twelve times in broad daylight. The journalist had written extensively about the negativity surrounding the drug trade. It is estimated that around forty journalists have been killed in Mexico since 1992. Six of those slayings happened from March to May of 2017.

In Russia, the dangers of reporting against President Vladimir Putin began to receive attention in the 1990s. In 2006, the journalist Anna Politkovskaya was murdered in an elevator in Moscow. Her death drew significant attention to the threats against Russian journalists. Reportedly, nearly twenty journalists have been recorded as being killed by the Kremlin. According to the *New Yorker*, "Nearly all the deaths took place in strange circumstances, and none of them have been successfully investigated or prosecuted." The Committee to Protect Journalists (CPJ) has found that more than fifty journalists have been killed in Russia since 1992. However, the CPJ notes the top three most censored countries are Eritrea, North Korea, and Saudi Arabia.

Another example of the power of the press came after the Republicans won the 2016 presidential election. Right before Democratic President Barack Obama left office, he said that Russia's president had hacked into the emails of Democrats. Obama said Putin then influenced the election by leaking those emails to the press. For whatever reason with all the negative news Trump received, people never had one negative word consistently tied to Trump. However, voters always remembered "email scandal" and "Hillary." The assumption is that this led to her losing the race.

"Every two years the American politics industry fills the airwaves with the most virulent, scurrilous, wall-to-wall character assassination of nearly every political practitioner in the country—and then declares itself puzzled that America has lost trust in its politicians."
—Charles Krauthammer, FOX News contributor and author

One thing Donald Trump did masterfully during the presidential primary campaign against sixteen other Republican candidates was to ensure control of each day's news cycle—often by making shocking statements. His view was to get himself good publicity each day, but if that was not possible, to get bad publicity. In doing so, he dominated the news day, preventing any of his opponents from getting a chance to make themselves part of the daily political discussion. Basically, Trump played the equivalent of ball control offense. As long as he could keep any of his opponents from having possession, they could not win.

In addition, there were analysts who compared what Trump spent on paid advertising, what his opponents spent, and what the equivalent dollar value of the coverage he got in the media was. Trump spent less out of his pocket than nearly all of his opponents, but the dollar value of "free" coverage for him compared to his opponents was off the charts.

Did You Know?

$1.2 Billion
Hillary Clinton spent $1.2 billion in her attempt to be the first woman President.

Breaking News

Half
For his successful presidential campaign, Donald Trump spent nearly 1/2 of what Clinton did.

$5 Billion
Trump earned $5 billion in free advertisement because he dominated the news cycle during the election.

After President Trump was elected he fired FBI Director James Comey. Comey then leaked documents about personal conversations between he and the president to the press in hopes that a special counsel would be appointed to investigate Trump's ties to Russia. It worked. The special counsel was appointed. The media's story also led to Comey testifying under oath before some members of the Senate. Comey was finally able to tell the whole world his true feelings in a controlled litigation style. The media continued to chew on that one as Trump responded, calling Comey a leaker and a liar. The significance here is that one of the most historic hearings on Capitol Hill all started because a former FBI director went to the most powerful entity: the press.

The media creates powerful results and even the biggest leaders of the world understand that fact. In 2013, former CIA employee Edward Snowden leaked a high volume of classified documents to the press. Some say Snowden is a criminal for leaking documents of national security. Others believe he is a hero. Either way, what is most significant here is that Snowden strategically ran to the press. He did not sprint to a lawyer. He did not track down the president of the United States. He went to the press to expose information to the masses. It worked. The news spread faster than an Olympian skier zipping down an icy slope.

Even at the local level, the press is seen as the most powerful entity. On March 28, 2017, the *Winston-Salem Journal* reported on the front page of the newspaper, "Councilmen buy stake in *Chronicle*." The story goes on to say that two African-American councilmen would now be the directors of a weekly paper that mainly served the African-American community. The general counsel for the North Carolina Press Association commented on the purchase, saying, "It is entirely up to the readers of the paper to decide what they think about it." A teacher of journalism ethics at UNC School of Media and Journalism also commented on the councilmen purchasing the *Chronicle*, "The folks who purchased it can say we are going to be fair and we are going to allow the journalists who work there to do their journalistic duty. But they are going to be faced with folks who are going to wonder if that is really possible."

Fake media has started to make its presence as well. For example, on Christmas Eve in 2016, a fake news story led the Pakistani Prime

Minister to threaten nuclear war against Iran. The fabricated news story falsely said Iran was threatening war. As a result, the Pakistani Prime Minister responded with a real threat of war. The fake news story was published on the website awdnews.com. The multiple typos and misattributed quotes beg the question, "What information is true and who authorized this fake news?" Luckily, the situation was corrected before real action was taken.

In April 2017, Germany decided to take a stance against the spread of fake news on social media sites. Social websites such as Facebook and YouTube can be fined up to $53 million with Germany's new law. Facebook, who has 29 million active users in Germany, noted to the press they are working with local companies to combat the fake news phenomenon. According to a report by Reuters, German politicians worry about the influence of fake news and reported Justice Minister Heiko Maas as saying, "There should be just as little tolerance for criminal rabble rousing on social networks as on the street."

Fake news does influence your thought process and emotions. Dr. Mehmet Oz of *The Dr. Oz Show* discussed the effects of fake news on the brain. During a study, Dr. Oz created two fake news stories. One was meant to rev up Republicans and the other to rile up Democrats. Neuropsychiatrist Dr. Daniel Amen assessed the brain activity of various women who read the false stories. One woman with liberal beliefs showed signs of sadness by the fake news story. The brain activity in the conservative woman resembled signs of physical threat by the fake news story crafted for her. Fake news stories do actually have the ability to make us feel despondent or susceptible to danger.

Even though the existence of fake news stories remains a problem, the true media still remains a powerful source. Accessing the press for financial gain, for example, can prove to be a mighty tool in the shed. Often times, the media acts as advertisement for you or your company without ever charging a penny. Just look at what the *Huffington Post* reported about Apple: "Nevertheless, the point remains: Apple can spend less on advertising than rivals like Microsoft and still get hype by just creating an information vacuum around its products and letting the hyperventilating media fill in the gaps around it."

Did you ever stop to think how and why certain stories appear in the press? For many, the irony of the timing of a breaking news story does cross their minds, but there is nothing to substantiate that thought. So the idea is pushed aside, the story is absorbed as truth, and the timing assumed to be a coincidence. It is seldom irony nor coincidence when Apple is in the news. The company is meticulous. Apple carefully plans their every move. Anyone looking for press should follow suit.

The press has access to millions of consumers collectively, who can help spread the word about you or your product. Even if your press coverage does not talk directly about your product, but promotes something positive about your business, you are getting your name out there, or the concept of what you are selling. People have a fascination with those who receive press. The news buzz about you will entice clients or buyers to notice you above your opponents. Just like a coach knows how to call the perfect play by reading the players on the basketball court, the press knows how to anticipate what consumers and constituents want to watch, read, or hear.

"According to the report, advertisers will have spent $72.09 billion on U.S. digital advertising by the end of 2016, while TV spending will account for $71.29 billion."

—*Forbes*

When someone sees an advertisement, he or she may question the motivation behind the advertisement and therefore question you or your product. Consumers buy based on word-of-mouth. The news is the best way to spread information to a mass amount of people at no cost. So when you get positive press, more cash stays in your wallet because money is saved on advertisement. Plus, once you are on the news, you can send the link to a consumer/client/buyer/voter. You can also send your news clip to other news stations proving you have been on the news and are a reliable source. Getting your foot inside the newsroom door provides you with credibility that makes you bigger and better than your competition. And wouldn't you like to beat your competition?

In Sir Isaac Newton's law of gravity, all objects attract each other based upon a certain gravitational pull. Newton's law of gravity could apply to the news and you. If you are a politician, the news needs you. If you are a subject matter expert, the news needs you. There will be an undeniable gravitational pull between you and the media. Why, then, is it hard to receive favorable coverage? Perhaps, the news has not heard of your story. As my eighth-grade English teacher, Mr. Michael Rewald, once said, "There are no boring things in this world, only things whose significances are not yet appreciated." If the thunder of your story has not been heard yet by a news station, I am assuming you did not present your story properly. If this is the case, you might wonder, what is the step-by-step process to accessing the media?

Here is the answer. There are certain ways to access the press and inform the public about the truth. There are also specific times when the media is hungriest for a news story. You want to strike accordingly. You will soon ascertain the art of how and when to strategically pitch a news story. As a result, you will maximize your own positive press coverage by putting on the full court press with our successful strategies. Once you do, you can share this book and your secrets with your friends. As a media expert, I too want to hear all about your success. Email me at: JillsMedia@gmail.com.

Chapter 2

Getting Press Coverage: A Behind-the-Scenes Look

A shley Papa is a network television producer in New York City and author of *Vixen Investigations*. As a producer at the top level, she has this advice:

> Utilize every media outlet out there. The Networks and big publications are obviously a huge deal, but there are also tons of local television stations, radio stations, podcasts, magazines, and papers all over the country. That saying, "go big or go home," doesn't apply because press is press and often, the big guys pick up the stuff from the little guys. . . . If nobody is getting back to you about your story it means they A. Aren't interested, B. Aren't interested right now, or C. It ended up in their clutter mailbox and they'll never see it. Move on.

While each news station is different, they are also very much alike. Knowing that, you can influence the media across the spectrum. It starts with local coverage first. Local stories can reliably lead to national attention. National media looks for stories in local outlets daily. It is through local media that you can get yourself state and national coverage. Cultivate your local media contacts. If you can influence the local media, you can be a top contender for the national media.

Why is it that local media controls the national media? Because the local media tests the story out to see how much traction your story picks up. If your story gains a significant number of viewers, the national media notices. The national media has not had to do the initial legwork of research. Nor has the national media wasted time discovering whether or not the story resonates with an audience.

What is newsworthy? Anything. It just depends on your pitch. I have seen local papers cover speakers at a Rotary Club meeting, just to fill the pages with pictures and encourage a sense of community. Keep a tally of which outlets are most willing to cover your story and track this with a chart. Then, you can refer back to it when you pitch another story.

For the general public, it's important to know what stories the media is presenting to you. When it comes to a headlining news story, there definitely is more than meets the eye. The list below is of great consequence. It provides inside access into the media's mind. Search online: "Most Popular News Stories." Immediately, sites like ABC, NPR, and *Forbes* will reveal a list of their most popular stories. If you have a good story related to the standard stories covered in the press like the list below, you will almost always receive media coverage. Whether you are raising funds for a charity, running for office, or simply interested in getting more press for your business, you can maximize your messaging goals by nurturing critical media relationships.

The Secret List of Top Trending News Stories

- Politics/Government
- Terrorism/Crime
- Flood, Famine, Fire
- Health/Medical Consumer Advice
- Community/Charity Events
- Weather/Traffic/Sports

The list is in no specific order because breaking news changes the order of importance. For example, an election can be the main headlines for a year. But then a big tornado could take over as breaking news which leads to ways in which people or companies are helping provide relief/charity. Another example is the Super Bowl. A couple of weeks leading up to the Super Bowl, I always pitch sports stories to the news department instead of the sports department.

Newsflash. Does your communications director know about the list of top trending news stories? You need to consider who you are hiring. For example, would you hire a veterinarian to operate on your heart if you needed a bypass? Never. You would hire someone with a specialized medical background to repair your heart to a robust state. The biggest mistake you can make is hiring a communications director or a political strategist with zero experience in a newsroom. You should be hiring someone with a reporter's background. Reporters have a few of the traits you need in order to personally connect with others. Plus, by using a former journalist on your staff or as a communications consultant, you gain access. Active reporters will naturally feel a kinship with someone they see as one of their own. If you cannot hire someone, this book will provide you with answers that will turn your story into positive press. Then you can share this book with others and provide your friends with insight as well.

Whether you hire a communications director or handle that function yourself, the key is to get out of the office and talk to people. Communications directors cannot do the job sitting behind a computer; they need to meet constituents and clients so they get to know their faces and hear their stories. That will give their press releases more passion and more heart, and those emotions will come across to the journalist.

What a Reporter Knows That Your Marketing/ Communications Director Does Not

Does a reporter wear high heels? I bet your communications director does not know the correct answer to this. The answer is no. A reporter is out in the field covering stories on foot—trudging through snow to get interviews, hiking through mud at a construction site, or walking through a crowd to ask for a quote. If your communication director does not understand this simple fact that reporters wear comfortable shoes, then your director might not understand a reporter's mentality.

A reporter's mentality: A scholarly reporter recognizes what story will be cast on the five o'clock news. He or she grasps this concept because they have fought for the lead story during the daily meeting. Why? Every good reporter wants to be the one covering the lead story. Subsequently, the reporter has learned which story will likely be the top pick of the day. In short, a reporter has come to realize what the viewers prefer to watch and consequently will make the top of the lineup.

Although this may seem crude, voters and consumers can be too lazy (or too busy) to fully examine all the choices. Most want one reason—not many—to reject or to continue to support a candidate or product. Hence, this is the reason why messaging is so crucial. Just one good takeaway in a story can give a voter or consumer the single reason they are looking for to make up their mind. And when that mind is made up, it does not usually change. To paraphrase a cliché, you only get one chance to make a lasting impression. That is why crafting your story to ensure the press reports it well is so crucial.

An experienced reporter with good instincts will know what stories touch the hearts of viewers. A solid reporter will know how to write and shoot video with incisive facts that touch the soul. Therefore, a press release written poorly, with boring facts that simply toot your own horn, will likely get turned down. In order to make the five o'clock newscast, your press release must entice the imagination of the person to whom you present it. It must be a story that touches the soul.

> "Even if Americans don't trust the government, they still want the government to do a whole bunch of stuff. . . . The vast majority (94 percent) [think] government should help keep us safe from terrorism."
>
> —*Washington Post*

While taking in complicated information, journalists must make the story emotionally compelling. They take out the jargon presented by the expert and replace it with words every average neighbor can relate to. I was once told I needed to write my news scripts with words that an eighth grader could understand. But I needed to convey emotion and visuals that pulled on the heartstrings of adults. Readers often won't remember the facts of the story; but if it's important to them, they'll remember the emotion they felt and the reaction they had. And once that occurs, the attitude formed at that moment is often cemented. Be cautious, though. That reaction needs to work for you, not against you, because of it permanence.

So when you see a news story, you often see comments from two sides: someone with a professional background who provides the facts, and a comment from an average person you might see walking down the street. The person walking down the street is the one who provides the emotional side of the story because he is more relatable to the average viewer.

Reporters try to shoot their video to show the soul of the story. In Al Tompkins's book *Aim for the Heart,* he talks about making an impression in a chapter titled: "Put a Face on the Story: You Remember What You Feel." People may not remember every aspect of the story, but they will remember how a person makes them feel. If your story on the news makes someone feel good, they will want to work with you. (Al Tompkins's website is also a great resource: aimfortheheart.com.)

As journalists, we are trained to focus on the heart of the issue and the soul of the story. As a result, journalists are observers of humans.

Reporters diligently dive into a subject matter, observe, and make an informed decision on how to report the story. Stories are not always cut-and-dry like a ninth-grade science experiment with a frog on the table. Therefore, the journalist learns about what viewers want to see and how to report accordingly, while also reporting the facts. It is the reporter's opinion on how to report the story based on the facts they are given and the scene they observe.

The Media's Bias

For those of you who say the media is biased, you are right. It is. Reporters and anchors are human. Humans, by nature, have an opinion. While covering a political race, they are deciding who they will vote for when they off the box on the ballot. While listening to a business, as a consumer, the reporter is deciding whether the product is good or not. It is human nature to think for ourselves. Reporters are not robots, nor should they be.

Many have asked me if I, as a journalist, have ever been biased. To say no would be saying I am not human. To be human is to be flawed. No human is perfect and God made every human to have an opinion. So while I certainly try to report fairly and have been extremely angry when I see biased reporting, I am sure at some point or another my subconscious kicked in and my reporting was not one hundred percent impartial.

Asking a reporter to be one hundred percent unbiased is like asking an employee to work one hundred percent every day. There are certainly fantastic employees just like there are brilliant journalists who work diligently with very little bias. However, it is impossible to give one hundred percent day in and day out. Sick days happen. Vacation happens. Triumphs and defeats occur in life which influence our behavior and work habits.

Do not get me wrong, reporters must focus on remaining neutral and reporting all the facts. They should cite two sources for every story. But because of deadlines and the intense schedule every reporter is under, sources are not always confirmed. The information you give them will not always be double-checked. Deadlines are always looming over the reporter like a clap of thunder looms over the heads of swimmers at a pool. Swimmers wait and wonder when the storm will approach. Reporters wait and wonder if they will get all the necessary information before a deadline approaches. If the information is not provided, a storm of events will occur—yelling, blaming, heavy sighs—leaving the reporter at the center of the storm for not doing his job on time. Therefore, sources are not checked or assumptions are made. The journalist must present the news and word is spread whether true or not.

Many journalists seek their news online. If the big story is from a news source who has been around for a long time, like the *New York Times*, the report is likely accepted as truth. Because who has time to check sources? There is a big deadline to think about instead. So while some anchors and reporters do an exceptional job of keeping their opinions at bay, many base their stories off of what has been reported online. This happens at the local and national level. Trust me.

However, not all journalists are lackluster in their research. Many try to make sure the truth comes out. Numerous reporters double check the story leak whispered in their ear. After all, it is the job of the journalist to seek the truth. Plus, all news outlets and reporters know if a lie seeps out of a story, a career and reputation is over. So journalists truly hope each story being reported is truth. Let me repeat, a journalist truly hopes the truth is reported.

Here is what you can do. Ease the reporter's workload as a parent would prepare a meal for a child. Make the editorial selection of the story easy for the journalist by providing what is needed: a story idea and great content. In doing so, you are providing the reporter with some fine dining. Your competitors may not do so, which leaves them idly sitting on the sidelines collecting dust. Often biases do not show up in the content of the story, but rather in the editorial selection of the stories. For example, the story may end on a positive quote you provided. Oftentimes, readers and viewers remember what they hear at the beginning and the end of the story. The middle of the story tends to get lost in translation. So if a reporter starts with a good quote from you, or ends on a good quote from you, the reporter is helping your case and perhaps showing some bias toward the story.

Reporters are experts at relaying facts in an enticing manner. A brilliant journalist clearly knows how to relate to a viewer's emotions, tug on the heart strings, and present the facts all at once. Just like Steven Spielberg knows how to draw a crowd to the theater with his movies, a good journalist knows how to tell a fascinating story filled with facts that ignite a strong emotion. For proof, look at any winner of the Pulitzer Prize. David Philipps from the *Gazette* in Colorado Springs, Colorado, is a great example. He won the national reporting category for covering issues surrounding the mistreatment of veterans who are discharged after being injured. Philipps wrote:

> Kash Alvaro stared at the ceiling of an emergency room in January listening to the beep of an EKG monitor for what he guessed was the 80th time in 12 months. The once-healthy Afghanistan War veteran had collapsed in a hallway that night, then awakened confused in an ambulance and lurched up in alarm, swinging and yelling until the paramedics held him down and injected sedatives.

Simply reading that quote immediately stirs up emotions of sadness for the veteran. Therefore, you want to be able to relate to the reporter who knows how to relate to the viewers. If you establish a connection with the reporter, you will be gaining rapport and trust with the reporter's audience. Therefore, it is imperative to cultivate an ally in the press.

In order to accomplish your goals, you must also be clear on your direction. Think about these three questions:

1. What information of yours do you want the news to cover?
2. What information of yours do the viewers need to know?
3. Where are you going professionally? If you want to keep climbing up the ladder, you need to tailor your media accordingly with local versus national.

For example, do you want to be the longest-serving mayor? Do you want to run the best restaurant in town? If so, we need to be heavy on the local media. Or, do you want to run for the Senate? Or do you want to grow your restaurant to become a national food chain? If yes, we need to focus on local and national news attention. (Then again, national exposure is welcomed adornment at any level.) Needless to say, your news exposure must be deliberate and strategic. There are three points of contact in which you can execute your goals and maximize your news coverage: before the event, at the event, and after the event.

Chapter 3

Three Points of Contact

Did You Know
some stations lack the man power to cover your story?

3 Points of Contact with the Press

Before the Event

1

Call the reporter and then follow up with a press release.

3

After the Event

Take photos or video at the event. Send it to the station immediately after the event.

2

At the Event

Greet the reporter and suggest people to interview.

If you want to gain positive media, you must think like the press. You must have at least three points of contact with the media: before the event, during the event, and after the event with a second press release. (Most people cut themselves short and only have one or two points of contact.) If you are extremely selective about what is presented before the press and when, instead of throwing a flurry of press releases in the reporter's lap, your odds of getting coverage increases.

The first point of contact is with a direct phone call to the press. In doing so, you are creating rapport with the reporter or the producer. You are finding out who you need to get in touch with directly, instead of sending a blind email. Once you find the correct person to contact, send a press release with pertinent information: who, what, when, where, why. The second point of contact is at the event. You want to greet the reporter and cameraman. Aid the reporter by telling her the names of important people at the event or people of interest to interview. Last, if the reporter does not attend an event, do not fret. Some stations want to cover your event but lack the manpower. Therefore, the last point of contact is to become the reporter yourself. Use your cell phone. Get some video, pictures, and interviews from your event. Send it to the station via email and let them know the details of the event. Sometimes, the station will use what you sent in and are glad for the extra news coverage.

By following these three points of contact with the media, you are not trying to just get a bigger share of a fixed pie; you are trying to motivate inconsistent voters, persuade consumers to support you or your product, or encourage volunteers to support your charity event. You can make that happen with good messaging and communication.

Unfortunately, a politician or communication director can be over-eager. He or she may send mass emails for every single event, hoping that at least one story will land. Do not try this mass email approach. Instead, you must learn when to move forward at the appropriate time and when to remain patient.

If you continue to take the mass email approach, your email will end up in the glance folder, as I like to call it. The glance folder is where the reporter subconsciously makes the decision he or she will likely not cover the story before the email is even opened. Out of obligation to be informed, the reporter clicks on the email with the tap of the thumb on the keyboard's mouse. The email is merely glanced over. The reporter thus confirms it was a waste of time. You never want your press release to be filed under that thought process. Remain composed in order to secure positive press during your newsworthy moment and attack during calculated opportunities.

The Newsworthy Moment

You must be creative and think about a different angle to a story so the news is eager to cover it. The news likes to stand up against bullies and defend the underdog. The news also likes to support local community programs, and this can lead to great opportunities for charity events.

For example: Let us say there is a family-owned landscaping company who runs a successful business. One of the sons is an Iraqi veteran. How can that family get publicity or find a newsworthy moment? An easy way is to hold a charity event, perhaps a 5K to raise awareness for soldiers suffering from post-traumatic stress disorder. Local news stations love to cover a charity event, especially one that is patriotic, and give it publicity. Weekend morning shows and noon shows will often have you on as a guest to promote the event. Then, you are raising money for a good cause and your company is getting publicity while doing it.

Here's a great example of a newsworthy moment: During the 2016 presidential race, Democratic candidate Hillary Clinton became the first woman to win the nomination of a major party. Some argued she was using her gender as a tool to gain votes. Her team intelligently responded with a clever and tactical retort that quieted her critics.

"If fighting for equal pay and affordable childcare and paid family leave is playing the woman card," said Hillary at a rally in Charlotte, North Carolina, "then, deal me in." Her team sent out emails of a photo of a pink card that said "Woman Card." It was literally Hillary's woman card that could be purchased by a supporter as a contribution. What a creative way to raise campaign funds!

Videos, photos, and sound bites are exactly what the press needs in order to produce a newsworthy story. The media is always looking for something to catch the viewer's attention. Whether it is during a moment of connection with a member of the crowd or through an informative tip, a reporter wants that one newsworthy moment that stands out.

Here is another situation for consideration: When Chelsea Clinton came to Wake Forest University to campaign for her mother, I attended the event. Chelsea talked about the importance of women attending college and college affordability. She repeatedly referenced the calculator on her mom's website for folks to utilize. It is no surprise Chelsea kept trying to convey this message because according to the *Winston-Salem Journal*, "Clinton's appearance came a day after her mother's campaign unveiled a college calculator on the campaign website that lets people figure out how much they could save under the Democratic candidate's plan."

However, one person from the crowd asked a question that stole the spotlight away from Chelsea. He was the lone wolf—a man in a room full of women.

"Sorry I'm not the right gender," he joked. "My question, ma'am is . . ." Then, he asked Chelsea a softball question. Chelsea quipped, "Oh no, he called me ma'am. That always makes me feel so old." The crowd laughed. The thirty-four-year-old young woman then adroitly responded to the question with ease.

Do you detect the newsworthy moment here?

The newsworthy moment is the issue of gender. After the event, CNN snatched up the man who asked Chelsea the question. He was peppered with questions about gender issues. Meanwhile, Chelsea's main message was sidelined. Why?—because the news outlets were looking for their newsworthy angle. (While national media tends to focus more on these types of controversial newsworthy moments to drive up ratings, local media tends to focus more on some of the facts of the speech. Therefore, you can more easily tailor your message to the local media, in hopes that the mainstream media will then pick up your concisely communicated story.) On that day, I gained a new understanding of the frustrations prominent figures have with the press.

But to keep friends in the news industry, you must work with the news industry. You must share information one on one. You will get more coverage that way and the news stations will appreciate you pitching them an extra story. In order to pitch a story with a newsworthy moment, you must think of a different angle.

In order to receive positive press, you must become friends with all press. To keep friends, you have to be a good friend. Just like you are going to be a good friend by sharing this book with a friend.

For example: Find someone who is truly affected by you or your product. Tell the news about that person. For instance, if I worked at Flow Auto, I would find a family in need of a new car but who cannot afford to buy one. Flow could then roll out the latest SUV and introduce the five family members to their new free car. The family could be interviewed and they would talk about how grateful they are to Flow. As a result, Flow is getting positive press while promoting their latest product. It is a win-win for all involved with great media coverage. (While I am sure you will appreciate the positive news coverage, you may feel even more joy from helping a family in need.)

> "I would rather excel others in the knowledge of what is excellent than in the extent of my powers and dominion."
> —Alexander the Great

Three Points of Contact

Once you are ready to flex your news muscles and contact the news stations in a way that will maximize your chances of getting media, remember to follow the three strategic points of contact:

1. **Before the Event:** Call the reporter and then email the first press release.
2. **At the Event:** Greet the reporter and suggest people to interview.
3. **After the Event:** You are the reporter—email a second press release with photos, video, facts, and quotes.

The following chapters talk in detail about each point of contact. One other point worth noting is the importance of tracking your success. As Tony Robbins says, "Success leaves clues." *Create a chart* of your success. Clue your colleagues in on what works for you and which news outlets give your team the most assistance. It will be a useful tool to refer back to each time you have a story to pitch.

Or use the insights in this book to create a calendar for your personal or professional campaign ahead of time. Set specific dates that you will send out your press releases, and decide who you will contact and when. Also note when you will follow up with each journalist. In other words, make a very specific game plan of dates and actions before your press releases start. Then follow it. Once you have accessed the media, I want to hear all about your success story. Be sure to email me, your media expert: JillsMedia@gmail.com.

MEDIA TRACKING CHART	
STORY:	NOTE THE STORY YOU PITCHED.
WHEN:	THE DATE YOU PITCHED IT.
NEWS OUTLET:	TO WHICH OUTLETS DID YOU SEND INFORMATION?
WHO:	NOTE THE CONTACT INFORMATION OF THE PERSON YOU REACHED OUT TO.
HELPFUL:	BE SURE TO NOTE WHO WAS HELPFUL AND WHO TO AVOID.
HOW:	HOW DID YOU PITCH THE STORY? WHAT METHOD WAS EFFECTIVE? WHAT WAS NOT?
SOCIAL MEDIA:	WAS ANY INFORMATION POSTED ONLINE IN REGARDS TO YOUR STORY? WAS THERE ANYONE REALLY HELPFUL IN SPREADING YOUR INFORMATION ONLINE?
FUTURE DATES:	DO YOU WANT FUTURE COVERAGE WITH THAT NEWS STATION? DO YOU NEED TO MAKE NOTE OF WHEN TO MAKE A FUTURE PITCH TO THE STATION?
LIST OF CONTACTS:	DID YOU MAKE NEW CONTACTS DURING THE INTERVIEW? BE SURE TO JOT DOWN YOUR NEW CONTACTS AND A SENTENCE OR TWO ABOUT THEM.

In the meantime, here is a sample Tracking Chart:

So many journalists agree with the three points of contact I teach you about in this book. Jeff Gravley emphasizes the importance of the third point of contact: becoming the reporter. Jeff is one of the people who votes for the winner of the Heisman Trophy Award, is a seven-time Emmy award winner, and has twice been named the North Carolina Sportscaster of the Year by the National Sportswriters and Sportscasters Association.

The following is his advice:

As a news organization, we get hundreds of e-mails per day from people and organizations pitching story ideas. There is no way we can fulfill all of the requests for coverage. The good thing now is sharing video is easier than it has ever been. Providing a short clip of a client on camera works much better that a written quote. It's better for television coverage as well as the web and social media. Working in sports, we sometimes get interviews and highlight clips of some of the non-revenue sports that we can't get to. It's a proactive way to try and get coverage. An invitation to cover an event can sometimes get lost in the shuffle. A follow-up e-mail immediately after the event that includes video is a good way to get noticed. It doesn't guarantee it will make air, but it increases your chances.

Chapter 4

The Inner Workings of a Newsroom

You saw a story on the news, heard it on the radio while driving to work, or read it in the newspaper. Here is a look behind the scenes that highlights why certain stories come to fruition. You will also note who you want on your side.

Behind the Scenes: Inside the Newsroom

If you search online for phrases such as "press office CNN" or "contact Today Show," you will find where to send your press releases. Each site has a generic place for anyone in the public to send his or her comments or press releases. However, if you want to increase your chances of getting on the news, you should contact folks individually. Of course, the anchor of the show is a great resource, but not everyone has access to the face in front of the camera. Therefore, you should look for those working behind the scenes who will also have influence.

Here are some of the people you want to search for online and why:

- *Booking Producer:* Booking producers utilize the book of contacts the news station has at its discretion. They book the guest for a show and ensure that all the travel arrangements are in line. It is a position that is usually given to a professional who has experience in the news but is not necessarily someone who has made it to executive producer status. So if the booking producer were on a basketball team, he or she would be a starter, but not necessarily your Michael Jordan.

- *Producer:* Producers are the editors and writers. They also pitch stories during the news meeting. Then, they write and edit segments for their assigned stories, confirm interviews, and print out research for the anchors who will use them to ask informed questions. The executive producer then double-checks the segments. (When you are booked as a guest on a show, you can provide the producer pages of your own research to be given to the anchor for your segment.)

- *Overnight Producer:* If you have an event at night, know which overnight producers are working. Overnight producers help put a story together for the morning shows. For example, the *Daily Caller*, the online newspaper whose editor-in-chief is Tucker Carlson, has an overnight producer. So the dayside producer will book stories. Then, if the reporter has to cover a story that night, the reporter will send the story into the overnight producer. The overnight producer will put all of the late-night stories together for the morning hours. You want to befriend these night owls. The overnight crew are usually extremely kind, too. It can be a lonely shift, so it is nice when someone appreciates your work.

- *Executive Producer:* Ideally, you want to pitch your idea to an executive producer because she is essentially the manager. She is the spine of the broadcast, connecting all the stories into one body. If you can make a personal connection with an executive producer, you have found a jewel to be stashed in your bag of connections.

- *Reporters:* The reporters cover the breaking news and are the hungriest for a fresh story. If you have breaking news, you will want to email the morning reporter, because they are always eager to have a fresh story to pitch at the daily news meetings. (Reporters are required to pitch a story among their peers. If you give them an exciting story, they will want to keep in touch with you.) Review the news station's website to see which reporter typically covers the political or business beat. As you might guess, the reporter beat does depend on the size of the station. The smaller the station, the wider range of topics a reporter will cover. The larger the station, say in Chicago or New York, the more available reporters. Therefore, reporters will likely have a specific beat. Either way, you will know which reporter to call because you will learn which reporter typically covers which beat. If the reporter covered your competition in the news, the reporter should get a quote from you. Contact the journalist and suggest you have a quote and can provide the opposing side's view.

- *Anchors:* The anchors are looking to pitch stories in the daily meeting as well. The anchors really care about the content of the show, because they will be talking about the content repeatedly for the various newscasts. So they are eager to make sure the stories are strong.

- *Assistant News Director:* Not all stations have assistant news directors. As you might guess, the bigger stations do. The assistant news director is like the assistant coach. He helps ensure the reporters and producers are executing their jobs properly. He can also fill in for the head coach, or in this case, the news director.

- *News Director:* The news director calls all the plays and decides which players will be on the court. The news director has the final say about how a show will be aired and what stories will be utilized. The buck stops with the news director.

- *Radio Hosts:* Cultivate relationships with on-air radio hosts. They need guests for their shows as much as you need the opportunity to speak to your audience. Become each others' best friend.

Just Know: A reporter or booking producer may not always pitch your story aggressively, especially if you have never received news coverage before. Even if you do have previous news appearances, your story may not be pitched with passion. I have had this happen to me from time to time. If you get turned down by a booking producer, go to your next contact. Most importantly, keep going back to your contact. People in the news may turn you down for one story but book you for the next two. And ask them—what's a guiding principle at your station for what you like to cover and what you don't like? They know who their viewers are and what they want, so find out what stories or story angles work best for them.

While the process to get in touch with the national news can be more arduous (unless you have an inside connection), local news—especially reporters—are desperate for you to get in touch with them. It is no coincidence that their email addresses and various social media accounts are typically posted on the station's website. And don't overlook contacting summer interns the paper or station might have used. They can be an eager source and excited to share their newfound insight on the interworkings of the newsroom.

At newspapers, reporters and producers work hand-in-hand. It is the top producer, though, who has the final say. For more behind-the-scenes information, refer to Chapter 10, which dives more in depth about newspapers.

Here's the bottom line: you have a list of contacts at your discretion online, any time, on any show. In our world today, folks love to connect with others and boast about their personal and professional achievements. Therefore, producers, reporters, and anchors will promote their careers on social media. Reach out to these individuals through social media. Alternatively, you can try to crack the email code. Consider that if you find out one person's email, the format is typically the same for all. For instance, you might see J.Smith@XYZnews for the producer. Thus, you might take an educated guess and suppose the anchor's mail would be a similar format, e.g., S.Jones@XYZnews.

Behind the Scenes: Ways to "Leak" to the Press

Keep in mind that the press is always looking for the next big story. Here are a couple of ways to notify them without directly disclosing yourself as a source.

1. *Have friends email the station a couple of days before sending a press release.*

   As you may recall, former FBI Director James Comey had his friend leak information to one reporter. Comey said he, himself, did not go to the press. If you do not have a contact at the national level, you can send emails to local stations such as: "Hi, are you covering this event?" Or, "Can you provide me details about the informational session being held about Medicare at the YMCA on Thursday?" Emails like these silently alarm the radars of producers and reporters of your event. (A reporter at a station I once worked for used to create fake email accounts to motivate the news director one way or the other. Few of our co-workers knew about the reporter's tactics, but the emails worked in a subtly, successful way. He was able to cover certain stories and even sent in compliments of stories he covered from a fake viewer.)

2. *Post the event on your website or social media pages a week in advance.*

   In mid-September of 2016, Trump used this tip before he held a rally at High Point University in High Point,

North Carolina. On his website, a note with information about the day, location, and date was posted. Local news directors and reporters were tweeting about the politician's appearance on their personal social media accounts before it was reported on the news, multiplying Trump's exposure.

When you do post to social media or the web, be short and concise. As Franklin D. Roosevelt said, "Be sincere; be brief; be seated." All too often, people get too wordy and the message is lost. Remember, less is more.

3. *Submit your event on the station's calendar of events a week in advance.*

On each station's website, there is a place to fill out information needed in order to be on the calendar. You would be amazed at how many people look at the station's calendar. Whether you are trying to leak information or not, I highly recommend you submit your events to various news calendars. It might create a buzz within the news station.

Behind the Scenes: Who Is Interviewed and Why

There are certain types of people interviewed on the news and there are specific reasons why the press will cover particular news stories. You can use both of these styles as ways to deliver the truth to the public. First, we will observe the two types of people interviewed by the news. They are:

1. *Subject Matter Expert:* A person who has credentials, experience, and knowledge on the subject matter being covered. The expert provides the viewer and station with factual information. For example, if there was a school shooting, the subject matter expert would be the sheriff

releasing information about the shooter being held in custody. Another subject matter expert might be a doctor updating us on the status of the victims in the hospital.

2. *Man on the Street (MOS):* An everyday person who is affected by the outcome of the story. The MOS humanizes the story. Let us use the school shooting example once again. The MOS would be a student or teacher in the building during the shooting. Another MOS might be a mother talking about what it was like getting text messages from her son who thought he would not survive the attack. The reaction from the MOS elicits the mood of the scene.

Here is another story to further illustrate the two types of people interviewed by the news. On March 23, 2010, President Barack Obama signed the Affordable Care Act into law providing health care nationwide. During the first year of enrollment, the news was covering various stories about the historical moment. As cofounder for Blue Bridge Benefits Insurance Agency, I was interested in our company accessing the press but also understood the importance of the public understanding this new, confusing insurance field. We wanted the viewers to know the truth about all the changes. We had so many calls with outraged clients, we needed to clarify the process.

Since we sold to people nationwide and I knew this historical health-care issue would affect people across the country for many years to come, we could inform many consumers and ease their minds better than a random advertisement. We could easily link our company to a story we knew the news would already be covering. I knew the news would need an expert to report on the inside knowledge insurance agents were receiving. We made sure to be that source.

Sure enough, a local reporter was interested and covered the story for their broadcast. The NPR radio station also gave Blue Bridge Benefits news time. They came to a booth Blue Bridge had set up at the mall for enrolling clients for Obamacare. NPR interviewed the agent on the spot. The agent had many folks contact him and say, "Hey, I heard you on the radio." Easy and free news exposure and promotion all because we initiated contact on a current news event. More importantly, it was truly informational. You could say it was a win for all: us, the news, and the viewers. And hopefully the viewers felt less angry or anxious about the new insurance changes.

Another time Blue Bridge Benefits received attention in the local paper was after one of the major carriers in our state announced insurance rates would be increasing. We knew this would affect a great deal of people. We toyed with the idea of putting an advertisement in the paper but knew folks would trust us more in a news story. We wanted to build more trust because there was already fear and angst about the insurance rate increase. Plus, it was more cost-effective to have a reporter write our story and tell our truthful ideas. We knew which reporter for the local paper covered the business beat. In fact, he had received awards for his writing. Therefore, the situation was explained to the reporter by a trustworthy source. In short, the reporter vetted us for his station's viewers. The story was well written. Another win for all.

Why Certain Stories Are Covered

Now that you grasp the concept of who is interviewed, you must understand why stories are covered. Whether reported at 5:00 a.m. or as breaking news at 6:30 at night, there are specific stories covered in the news. Here are the reasons why:

- *Certain stories are covered because they are the most important headlines of that day.* It is difficult to anticipate if your story will be the best story of the day. It could be, but it will depend on what information is coming into the news outlet and the order of importance the decision-maker assigns to the stories.

- *Certain stories are covered because there is very little news to cover that day.* You might get lucky. Sometimes, your story could be last on the list. Other times, it could be first. Your story may be considered of no importance one day, but the best option on a slow news day. You never know until that day.

- *Certain stories are covered because they tie into other headlines.* There are particular times when you can capitalize on opportunities. Be on the lookout for stories relating to your area of expertise. Politicians especially have an advantage with the media, because the media feels like they are the fourth branch of government. They report the truth to the people and hold others accountable in the public court. Whether you are a politician or not, it is important to be strategic about what information you want to push to the news outlets. Before contacting a news station, you should check the most up-to-date headlines of the day. Check the headlines of local and national news, in print and on television. You are searching for ways to make your story relevant to the headlines being covered that day. Find stories in the news that relate to your issues.

  Next, weave your story into the current news. You don't always need to make news; you can instead demonstrate how you are already an active part of the news. Once you find a way to link your story into the current trends being covered, start reaching out to various news stations individually. There are so many news outlets from radio and TV to print and online papers. One of them should pick up your story.

For example: If there is a protest about the Second Amendment and you are trying to promote gun control or own a gun shop, you should contact the news station and tell them you have another angle that relates to the headlines. Not everyone will take the bait your line is casting, but if you have a good story, someone should get hooked. If you have a really good story, many news outlets will have to bite. They will not want to miss out on a good news story. Hence the reason you will see many news outlets at one press conference. It is too big of a story to pass up.

Always make sure when speaking to the press, or even when it's covering your story, to work in one comment designed to be the quote the press uses. Whether giving an interview or speaking at a public event, remember that the press will select the quote that works best for their story, not yours, so make sure that you have a quotable phrase somewhere in the content of your remarks that seems like the lowest hanging fruit for the reporter. And of course, make sure that one remarkable comment is the message you want your readers to have as their single impression of you. For example, John F. Kennedy gave a long inaugural speech, but his speechwriters gave him one line that was clearly crafted to be the one repeated in later press: "Ask not what your country can do for you, ask what you can do for your country."

Chapter 5

First Point of Contact: Before the Event

People like people who are like them. When servers repeat orders, customers subconsciously feel that the server is more like them than not. People who are in good rapport mirror each other's gestures and speech.

—*Psychology Today*

According to *Psychology Today*, when a waiter repeats an order back to a customer, the customer feels reassured by the verbal confirmation. It elicits good rapport, to repeat another's wants and needs. A waiter can also receive a bigger tip by leaving a material object, like a mint. If we receive something from someone, we feel obligated to reciprocate in kind. Have you ever been invited to a cookout by a friend and consequently invited that friend to your next dinner party out of obligation? You did so because of the law of reciprocity. We reciprocate the actions of others whether on an emotional or material level. People in the news are no different. Journalists will likely reciprocate your actions, as long as you are a reliable source, which means a truthful source.

Calling the Station

If possible, make a phone call first to create a good rapport. Abraham Lincoln said, "A drop of honey catches more flies than a gallon of gall." Use a drop of honey with journalists. Reporters and producers are human. On a conscious or subconscious level, a reporter may help you depending on the rapport you create. Therefore, it is important to make a phone call first to create a connection. Send a press release second. Sending a press release without a phone call or creating rapport is like sending a blind man into a lion's den. The odds of the press release surviving are slim.

How to Create a Connection: Check Two Places before Your Call

1. *The station's website.* The website gives you knowledge of what stories are being covered at the station that day. As a result, you can make your pitch relevant to the stories of the day.

2. *Social media.* Wouldn't it be nice to know a reporter or producer's true feelings before that first phone call? You already do. You know a newsperson's true feelings based on what they post on their personal social media sites. The social media page gives you inside access to what the reporter or producer likes or dislikes. I've even seen social media accounts where producers or anchors post a disclaimer in the "About Me" section saying, "Any comments I make on my site does not reflect those of this news station." It may not reflect the place where you work, but if you are a Democrat and I am a Democrat, I will be able to get on your show easier. Likeminded people like to help each other out—another reason the media is biased. It is just a fact of life.

For example: If you go on Savannah Guthrie's Twitter account, you will notice the NBC morning anchor has over 480,000 followers. But, she only follows less than nine hundred people, including Vice President Joe Biden and the former presidential Republican candidate, Marco Rubio. That she is tracking these people is not too surprising since Savannah needs to be updated on politics as an anchor. (Now why would she do that? Perhaps, she thinks they have future plans and she wants to be the first to know them.)

However, Savannah also follows a lot of tennis folks such as Roger Federer and Chris Evert. Do you think NBC's morning anchor is a tennis fan? She is. On September 2, 2015, she tweeted a picture of her daughter watching the US Open on TV and wrote, "We all love tennis in this family."

You can use this information as a way to strike up conversation. "Hey, did you see that match yesterday?" Or "I just got tickets to a big tennis match but can't make it. Are you interested in taking my tickets?" There are ethics rules about politicians accepting gifts, but there are none for those in the press.

I cannot emphasize enough how important it is to call the reporter at the station. In addition to creating rapport, it gives the reporter the chance to hear the passion in your voice—something emails cannot always portray. Very few people put the time and effort into a phone call—especially in today's technological age. But if you call each individual reporter, your chances of getting on the news increases. Take the time. Make the call. But do know, when you talk to a reporter on the phone it is essentially a mini-interview. The reporter is not only asking you questions to get information about your event, but also deciding whether or not you would sound intelligent on camera, on the radio, etc. As a morning news anchor, there were many times I'd chat with a person over the phone who sounded extremely knowledgeable. But as soon as the person was put in front of bright lights and cameras, he would give boring, brief answers. That in turn, made my job more difficult. I now had to get more creative with my questions on air to get the answers I previously heard while talking over the phone. Consequently, I soon learned to get better at fielding the callers with mini-interviews.

If you call to talk with a specific reporter and she is not there for the day, kindly ask which reporter is most likely to cover a story about business, or politics, etc. Or, ask for the producer in charge or editor in charge. But calling is the best option by far. It puts you in direct contact with the person most interested in your story. I suggest you call between 8:30–9:00 before the morning meeting. Or a phone call between 1:30–2:00 before the meeting for the evening news would be beneficial. (You will quickly learn the best time to call.) Then shoot your press release in an email right after your conversation.

Sample Conversation to Create Rapport with a Reporter

In order to create the necessary and respectful relationship with a reporter, here is what one might say:

"Hi Jonathan, it's Jill. I saw your report on job growth and the importance of shopping local. Very informational." (Find something that genuinely impresses you. Your compliment must be sincere. Also, by complimenting the reporter about a former story, you are notifying him how you have observed his reports. A journalist wants to make an impact. A journalist likes to know his stories are spreading and that the hard work is paying off.)

"Oh thanks," says journalist Jonathan.

"If you are not too busy, I would like to email you the details about a story. Are you interested?" (Reporters are always interested. This way, you have him saying "Yes," which hopefully entices him to say "Yes" to your story idea.)

"Sure," Jonathan says. "What is it about?"

"Recognizing the future leaders of America. One of the kids had the world stacked up against him, but defied the odds. I'll send the details shortly. But first what are you guys covering today? Anything on the calendar?"

"Sounds like a good human interest story. The Fire Department is having their annual practice series. They are putting out a fire and delivering CPR on dummies. We'll also probably do something on back-to-school stuff," says Jonathan.

"Interesting. Our story may tie into the back-to-school story since we are recognizing boys in high school. What time is your meeting to pitch stories? I want to get you the information before you guys sit down." (Reporters are always on a deadline. Here, you are being courteous of their timeline by asking when the reporter needs the email. Journalists always appreciate this because not everyone is respectful of a reporter's chaotic, daily deadline. Plus, you are putting the reporter in control. A reporter also appreciates this because a reporter is always waiting on everyone else's schedule in order to put his story together.)

"Right away would be great because I can have a story to pitch in the morning meeting," notes journalist Jonathan. "I had nothing to pitch. There's not a lot of news right now." (Every reporter must pitch a story among his peers at the daily meeting. The more stories the reporter has to pitch, the better the reporter looks in front of his peers and boss. You are aiding the reporter at his job.)

"No problem. Also, I know Chief Brooks at the fire station. Do you want me to ask him if there are any interesting angles to the fire story? Also, are there any other people you have tried to get in touch with for a story but who are not commenting?" (Here you are letting the reporter know you are a willing and helpful resource. If you can help the reporter, the reporter will be more willing to pitch your story in the meeting. You are working together as a team.)

"I probably don't need help with the fire story, but I have been trying to get in touch with the Governor's office about the proposed budget. Do you know anything?" he asks. (Most likely, Jonathan has already made this phone call, but he is hoping an insider like you can make more headway.)

"Let me make some calls and see what I can find out. I'll shoot the email with your story for the morning meeting first. Then, once I find something out from the Governor's office, I can get in touch with you." (If you agree to go the extra mile, you must uphold your promise. You must also do this swiftly. Hang up the phone with Jonathan, email the press release, and pick up the phone again to call the Governor's office. If the Governor's office gives you no new news, Jonathan will still appreciate you making a phone call to find out. Plus, it is one more excuse to follow up with Jonathan, check to see if your story will be covered, and develop better rapport. Additionally, if you report back quickly, this will also be added to the plus side for you in journalist Jonathan's mental file.)

Behind the Scenes: The Perfect Press Release

Step 1: Call the Reporter

Step 2: Email a Press Release: Your press release is basically like a resume. You present a resume at a job interview to show why you are a worthy candidate. You submit a press release to show the news why you have a worthy story. Thus, your press release is extremely important. There are certain steps you can take to earn a gold star in the press release world. (Sample press releases are included in the back of this book.)

Here is a general rundown of how to craft your press release:

- *Keep the Email Subject Line Simple:* Statistically speaking, the fewer words in a subject of an email, the more likely a person is to open it. Thus, the subject of every email should be: "Reporter's Name—Story Idea." Anyone in the news is always looking for a story idea. Every TV or radio reporter wants to have his or her story be the first one breaking in the newscast. Every reporter for a newspaper wants his or her story to be the one on the front page. If this happens in either news outlet, it is a sign the reporter scored the best story of the day. The lead reporter is much like the quarterback throwing the winning touchdown. The reporter is hoping your story will be that throw to victory.

- *Provide Statistics:* Statistics engage the reporter and station. It should be submitted in bold at the top of the press release. Because statistics can be such a powerful way to convey the importance of the story or event, a reporter will likely also be using them in his story to engage the audience. By providing statistics right at the reporter's fingertips, you are making the reporter's job easier, which increases your odds of getting in the news. Remember, make your story the reporter's path of least resistance that day.
- *Use National News:* If the national news has covered this story, use a quote from that outlet followed by your statistics. Let the media know this is a story affecting many people here and throughout the United States.
- *Use Video:* Provide the reporter with a video of you in the news from a prior news story if you have one. Hopefully, the reporter will see how intelligent you sound in the news, making you a more credible source for him. If you want to provide the reporter with a quote, your press release necessitates a video quote. It is better than a written one. It is more entertaining. Plus, television stations want to know you can talk intelligently on camera. Even a simple video with your cell phone can provide this in five sentences or less.
- *Put a Face with the Story:* It is most important to include photos of those who are affected. To get remarkable results, you must make the focus of the news release about the person or persons affected by your actions. Always find a face or photo to go with your story. Let us say, for example, you are a politician and just passed a bill that affects college kids. Find a college kid your bill will help. Attach his photo, showing him studying and smiling.

    Your headline for the press release could be: "Mark Burger is working toward affording his dream—the first to graduate from college." That's a much better headline than, "Politician Haggerson is hopeful his education bill will pass in the Senate." Which report would you rather watch? The story about the politician trying to get publicity for his bill? Or would you rather see the story about the motivated kid who would go to college if this education bill passes? Which one will you most likely relate to?

- *Include Graphics:* If you cannot include a video or photo, do include a graphic or infographic addressing the point you are trying to deliver. Remember the old adage, "A picture is worth a thousand words." It is true. You must have some type of visual to go with your message. For example, view the infographic below.

- *Avoid Jargon:* Do not assume your audience knows as much as you. But do provide reporters with links they can easily click on for more information. Try to provide those links all in one area, perhaps at the bottom of the press release. That said, keep in mind not to write paragraph after paragraph about your subject matter. Either attach a word document with more information or provide a link. (It is important not to inundate the journalist.)

- *Be Concise:* Keep the first press release short by providing information in the sacred five journalist categories: who, what, when, where, and why. Knit the words tightly together with the same impact a seasoned poet might. For instance, when writing down the "Who," do not put your name down. Everyone does this. But the real story is not about you. It is about the people who you will affect. The news consistently covers the people who are affected because those are the people watching the news.

- *Include Contact Information:* Include information for those faces you are putting with the story. You want to make it easier for anyone trying to confirm your story.

- *Make Sure Your Grammar Is Flawless.* You lose credibility if you cannot present a well-written press release. If possible, get someone you trust to look it over with a fresh eye. He or she may catch what you have already looked at ten times and become desensitized to.

Does the above information seem overwhelming? Look at the graphic below. It is almost the same information. Does it seem easier to read? Is it more enticing? The graphic takes the information from above and breaks down the jargon. The illustration is a perfect example of how to entice a reporter with concise information by using a simple graphic.

PRESS RELEASE
CHECKLIST

1 Email
*The subject of every email sent should say: "Reporter's name--Story idea." A journalist is always looking for a good story idea.

2 Statistics
Use statistics to tell why your story is important.

3 National News
If national news is covering a similar story, quote the national news at the top of your press release to give your story validity.

4 Video
Provide your quote in a video or attach a video of you on the news addressing a similar topic.

5 Photo
Always provide a photo to put a face with a story. You are humanizing the story.

6 Graphic
If you don't have a photo, provide a graphic, especially if there are numbers involved.

7 Avoid Jargon
Do not assume others are as knowledgeable as you. Simplify the information.

8 Be Concise
Keep the first press release short by providing information in the five categories: who, what, when, where, and why.

9 Contacts
Include contact information for everyone involved in the story.

10 Grammar
No grammatical errors.

Sample Press Release

Here is a sample press release that you could send to journalist Jonathan, with whom you talked to earlier. Let us say your story is about you recognizing the Eagle Scouts in your area. Rather than talking about how you are giving awards, talk about the Eagle Scouts. This bears repeating: put *their* faces with the story. Not yours. The news will be more likely to cover it because that is how the news would cover the story. It will appeal to their audience. Remember, if you think like the news, you will get your story in the news.

> *Famous Eagle Scouts: Neil Armstrong, Michael Bloomberg, and former President Gerald Ford.* —USscouts.org
> *"The total percentage of senior class presidents that were boy scouts: 89%. The total percentage of FBI agents: 85%."* —StatisticBrain.com

Who: Eagle Scouts

What: Eagle Scouts are being recognized by Congresswoman Jane Doe for their high achievement.

When: Today at 3:00

Where: The Civic Club at 300 Main Street

Why: From Cub Scout to Eagle Scout, these boys are the future leaders in our schools and in our community. This rank is achieved by only 4 percent of all scouts. You may also want to meet Eagle Scout Scott Smith, who defied all odds and beat cancer at a young age. Today, he is cancer-free and an exemplary leader.

Attached are photos of each Eagle Scout who will receive the recognition. Also attached is a video of Congresswoman Doe commenting on the importance of recognizing our future leaders.

Contacts: Eagle Scout Leader Bob Smith: Bob@1234gmail.com (212) 555–1212

Links for More Info: www.EagleScouts.com

Did you see how I made the story personal? It talks about the importance of Eagle Scouts, as well as one Scout in particular to pique interest. Yet, Congressman Jane Doe's name was quietly tucked in there. She will be the source of expertise. As a result, she provides a video comment that was filmed with her on her cell phone. The reason she provided this was so the news could observe her as she talks, looking on the ball and capable on camera. (Remember, the news wants to make sure they don't have someone who will freeze when the interview begins.) Therefore, Congresswoman Doe will be in the story and receive positive press.

In the press release, the statistic highlights just how unique and special this achievement is, making it worthy of the news. Next, a statistic that pertains to school is provided. You told journalist Jonathan you had a story that would tie into education. By linking the stories together, the odds of your story being covered increases.

But why link stories? Because news stations like to connect the dots between stories like a long chain. Each story is a chain link connecting to the other. The more potential links provided, the easier to find an easy transition. You can tell when an anchor is finished linking stories because she may something like, "In other news . . ." She may also say, "Now to a story affecting the hearts and minds of many." In doing this, the anchor is preparing the viewers for the type of emotional story that will come next.

Thus, an anchor could easily transition from the back-to-school story to your story. The anchor could say something similar to this: "And speaking of back to school, some local boy scouts earned their Eagle Scout badge before hitting the books. As our own reporter, Jonathan Rogers tells us, Eagle Scouts tend to be among the class leaders. And perhaps, even future leaders in America." (You could even send a sample transition to the reporter, if you have a comfortable relationship.)

No matter the relationship, always be sure to send the press release individually to each station. So few people capitalize on this opportunity. Almost all send mass emails. Do not vacillate on this endeavor or became apathetic about this strategy. I repeat: *Never send mass emails.* Since you are calling each station to find out the individual stories of each station, an individual email is warranted for your story pitch. Your success rate will rise if you individualize your news contacts. Also, make sure you only send information pertinent to the news outlet.

Let me mention again that I will put someone's name in the subject line of emails to try to help ensure that my reader will read it, e.g. instead of using "Story Idea" in my subject line, I would use "Jill Osborn—Story Idea." I'm trying to make Jill think this is a personalized message to her. I'll do thirty of those individually by copying and pasting the content, rather than one email to thirty people. Takes a little more time, but you can do that thirty times in thirty minutes. Seems to work. By my responses, I think I get twenty-nine of thirty to read it, instead of twenty-nine of thirty to ignore a mass mailing. (See how I used that telling statistic to back up my advice?)

Let us consider the following example: Say one Eagle Scout is from the town of Clemmons and the other four are from Winston-Salem. Then, only send the picture of the Clemmons boy to the *Clemmons Courier Newspaper* when sending them a press release. Send the picture of the other four Winston boys to the *Winston-Salem Journal.* You must tailor the press release according to the needs of each news medium. You will get more coverage if you take the time to do it. Photos help tell a story. Do not inundate a reporter with multiple photos that he must sift through. Only send the necessary information. The reporter is more likely to cover your story if he is not overwhelmed or if your story is not more time-intensive.

What to Know As You Pitch Your Story
Here is some information that may embolden you to present the truth to the press:

1. *Fear Not.* I have seen a lot of politicians and successful business owners who will not capitalize on being in the news because they fear it. They worry about what might be printed or televised. If you have a good story to tell, you need not fear how the reporter will spin it. If you know the reporter and see how he or she operates, you will learn the reporter is not necessarily always trying to trip you up, but simply trying to relay a really good story.

2. *The press is cautious.* There is trepidation on the news side as well. As a reporter, it was ingrained in me as if etched in stone with a hammer and chisel—make sure to report the facts. News stations always fear the possibility of being sued in slanderous lawsuits. More importantly, perhaps, they guard their trustworthiness. For example, I saw one paper have all the facts about a story with documents from a court case, but they were hesitant to print the story before another news outlet. They were concerned about a slanderous lawsuit and injuring their credibility factor. Ultimately, the paper printed the story and nothing came of it but heart palpitations from the politician being written about. But the significance here is that all news mediums have a fear of commenting on a story first.

3. *Gifts are welcomed.* Remember the old maxim about catching more bees with honey? When I was the morning anchor for the ABC affiliate in Nebraska, we loved having a local restaurant on our midday show because they would always bring us free food. The entire staff would have a free, delicious lunch, and you better believe we were happy to invite them back on the show. Many journalists appreciate such kind gestures. Whether it is ethical or not, I have seen it happen in my industry time and time again. Why is that? Because they are human beings. They are performing the

art of a thankless, competitive job during horrible hours. It is nice to be thanked.

4. *Go in and meet the news directors, news editors, and people in charge.* Take them out for coffee or a bite for lunch. If you are a good source, they will want to keep a working relationship with you.

5. *Give off-the-record information.* Be selective about the information given and see whom you can trust. If indeed the newsperson is trustworthy, keep that ally. In doing so, you are forming fortitude of partnerships. The inside ally will become your leader in pitching story ideas at the news meetings. That can help with any future stories you have, as well as keep the lines of communication open. Additionally, you are showing those at the news stations you are a trusted source. As Mark Twain once said, "An honest man in politics shines more there than he would elsewhere." The same works for news sources.

6. *Before an in-studio interview, offer extra footage of yourself to the producers.* The extra video can be of you working at your desk, or talking to clients or constituents—shots that are pertinent to the story. Always have extra video of you so that you can provide the reporters with extra footage. Television reporters will always need extra video. However, do make sure the video is specific to the reporter's needs. It makes no sense to send video of you driving a car if the journalist is writing a story about voter fraud. If you cannot provide video that is relevant to the story, at the very least, provide photos. (For more information on how to record video, read Chapter 11.)

7. *The news is a competitive business.* News stations are competitive. Every news station wants to be the first to break a story. If it is a good story, other stations will want you to comment on their show as well—even if other stations have

already covered it. Journalists do not want to be scooped or look as if they do not have the same access to the VIP moment. Smaller news stations will typically follow each other. So make sure if you are on one local station, you are on them all. For example, I have seen different stations interview the same person on the same subject matter one at noon and the other at 12:30. With some of the bigger networks, however, you may want to take the opposite approach. Instead of trying to go on every show in the viewing area, offer an exclusive interview to one station.

8. *Got advertisements?* In local media, and especially in national media, it is important to have an ally on the inside willing to fight for your story. Unfortunately, in the media world, creating an ally can happen by giving money to the news outlet. If you can cough up the dollars, the news outlet will help you out. In fact, while I will not name the source, I have seen a person receive press simply because that person donated money to the station through advertisements. This is not hearsay. It just shows how the media can fall prey to bias. (I was told to interview a certain person by a salesman in the sales department. Our show was already booked and I did not think it was fair to give the person extra air time just because he paid our station for commercial space. The general manager politely insisted I do it. As a young journalist, I felt I had no other option to concede.)

   It is your choice whether you want to throw money at a news outlet or not. In my opinion though, cultivating a more ethical relationship far outweighs the financial approach. It will enable longer lasting friendships, with greater results, while keeping cash in your wallet.

9. *Don't go for the hard sell.* Jim Williams is an award-winning journalist who has reported around the world for *Good*

Morning America, World News Tonight with Peter Jennings, and *Nightline.* He is currently a reporter and anchor for CBS in his hometown of Chicago, and offers this final piece of advice for press releases: "Do not tell us how many other media outlets are promising coverage or how many stations/websites/newspapers have already covered your story. People are unlikely to respond to that kind of pressure."

Jim's other tips serve as good reminders:

- Personally address the media member you're trying to reach; "Dear Jill," etc. A blanket email is more likely to be ignored.
- Ideally, cite that media's member's work. "I enjoyed (was moved by, respected) your report on the young man who returned to his high school as principal." It shows you've done some homework.
- Follow up with a phone call.
- Keep the pitch short (reporters, managing editors, producers are swamped with pitches these days).
- Place a human being in the center of the pitch. Who benefits, has a problem, is doing something great? Make it personal, not abstract.

Chapter 6

Timing: When to Contact Each News Outlet

Do what you can, with what you have, where you are.
—Theodore Roosevelt

An Easy Way to Get Coverage: Ever watch a freezing reporter cover the snowy weather as you watch the report in your warm house sipping on a hot cup of cocoa? If so, get up and get out there. If you feel safe enough to do so, drive around during inclement weather. Take photos and cellphone videos of downed trees, sagging power lines, or of kids sledding. When there is bad weather, the news never has enough eyes out in the field covering the scenes. Send those photos and videos into the station. Call in and offer to do a "phoner" where you describe what you see while driving around downtown or various neighborhoods.

You can even let the reporters know in advance that you will be there so that they know to look for you with their pen and pad, microphones, or cameras. Nine times out of ten, you'll be there while everyone else is sitting at home with their hot cocoa.

You can also call into the station and ask the reporters where they will be covering each report. Likely, they will go live in various viewing areas. Ask them if they need an interview, or just go meet the reporter at the location. It is challenging for a reporter to find an interview during inclement weather, but you can add a different dimension. You can describe to the reporter and the viewers what the drive was like on the way in.

Receiving Big Press in a Big Way

When news breaks, the producers are trying to keep up with the pace of the fast news. Contact a station immediately if you can comment on a national story. Call them to say you are an expert in the field and have insight into the subject matter. When covering a national story with a local spin, it is called localizing a national story. Local news stations do not always like to do this, but some do.

For example: Let us take the story about Captain Sully Sullenberger safely landing the plane on the Hudson River. I know a business owner who sells security devices to homes. However, as a hobby, he has his pilot's license. If I were him, I would contact the news outlets and tell them, "I have my pilot's license and can comment on this story or answer any questions about the logistics if you need some answers." Therefore, you are putting a local spin on a very popular national story. You are also linking yourself to a heroic story. You are also subtly advertising your business because you will be introduced as John Doe, owner of Engineer Tech, who is also a pilot. Once you do this interview, you have formed a relationship with the news. You can continue to do more interviews and direct your pitches toward your business.

If you pitch a story and land a spot on the national news, notify your local media stations immediately, so they have an opportunity to cover your story, too. This especially applies to politicians. Even if you become a regular guest on the national news, notify your local stations. Tell them: "MSNBC is covering this story and I am commenting on the subject. I can comment for you as well." It is important to notify the hometown news teams for two reasons: First, the news outlet will be glad you are keeping them up to date; because, truth be told, it is their job to be in the know. However, no one can have eyes and ears everywhere. Second, if you keep your hometown team in the loop with your news debuts, you will likely get more local coverage. If you get more local coverage, more national stations will notice. The endless cycle of your news coverage begins.

Whether you are strategic enough to link a story to the headlines of the day or not, it is important to plan ahead. Think quality. Never quantity. As a reporter, I have received two press releases for two separate events from one political office. The problem was the press releases were emailed within minutes of each other. While the events were on Monday and Thursday, it was still the same story: about the Congressman. I need variety.

Rather than inundating a reporter with every little possible story, look at your calendar of events. Choose which events are newsworthy. Submit a press release to one reporter to cover event A. Submit the second press release to a separate reporter to cover event B. You could also choose a television reporter to cover story A and a radio reporter to cover story B. Now, you are tapping into a different set of audiences.

It is so important to be selective and highlight which events you want covered. What message do you want relayed to the public? If you are not strategic about your branding, some of your emails will go into the news spam pile. None of your emails should ever go into the spam pile, because reporters should regard you as a newsworthy wealth of information.

Timing in the National News World

The morning anchors and producers have a grip on what will be going on that day. Stations like NBC, MSNBC, FOX, and CNN have producers working overnight in order to keep a pulse on the worldwide news and what information is breaking.

When are guests booked for the show?

Each station is different, but typically morning shows book the day before or in advance, depending on how big the event is. If you want to be on a national morning show, the time to contact the station is right after the show is over. They have their morning meetings after the show with the executive producers. So if you have an event on Wednesday, you want your story pitched in the morning meeting on Tuesday. (Typically, all shows have a meeting after their shows to discuss what worked, what did not work, and what's on the schedule for the next day and week ahead. However, if you want to be on a national show and need to make time for travel arrangements, contact the station earlier in the morning a couple of days before your event.)

While the morning shows must book in advance, evening news has more flexibility. Evening and day shows book guests the day of the show or days in advance. While they prefer to book the guests in advance (as opposed to scrambling around at the last minute), producers understand that news breaks. Therefore, guests may have to be scheduled even a couple of hours before the show.

The evening news is packed with stories because they have been able to follow the headlines of the day. They have more time to prep for the show during daytime hours when folks are available to be booked or filmed in advance for a video report.

A couple of hours prior to the daytime or evening shows, the anchors are studying the material they will be covering on the show. They have packets of information about each segment that will air, along with additional research the producer has found. This is also about the time anchors get their hair and make-up done. Therefore, the ideal time to contact the anchor or reporter is at least five hours before the show, unless you have a story that you can tell them about in advance that relates to pertinent headlines.

As you can imagine, all shows prefer to book guests earlier—even up to a couple of weeks in advance, depending on the event. For example, before Hillary Clinton and Donald Trump had the most-watched televised debate with 84 million viewers tuning in, the news was lining up commentator's weeks in advance. They were booking political pundits for their Tuesday show (the day after the debate).

Timing in the Local News World

Depending on the number of employees, typically producers and anchors arrive in the morning for local news stations around the same time. Not every station has overnight producers. The number of employees all depends on the market size of the station. But when the morning producers and morning anchors begin working on the show, they are typically rewriting and reusing last night's news from the 10:00 p.m. newscast. This is done, in part, because there is not a lot of overnight news happening at local stations. Also, they may not have the manpower to cover overnight news. (Plus, folks who watch the late-night news are not usually up watching the morning news and vice versa. Thus, some stories are repeated and no one really grumbles.)

The morning producer and anchor do, however, call the local police station, sheriff's department, and fire department to see if there was any big news overnight to report. Local morning shows are always looking for new content. If you have new content, you can talk with them as early as 3:30 a.m. Rise and shine!

The evening news, though, is chock full of new information because the world has been buzzing around all day. As a result, the staff is typically bigger for the evening shows than for the morning shows because there are more pertinent stories to go out and cover. The evening staff will typically show up around 2:00 p.m.

There are certain times when a news outlet is more receptive and eager for a news story. Therefore, when you send a press release, it is important to time each one out to perfection. You must notify each news outlet according to when your news story is needed the most.

When to Send in Your Story

Know how much time is needed before a deadline. Newspapers, radio, and TV are different, and it is crucial to tailor your story accordingly.

Newspapers

A deadline for a newspaper is written in stone. The paper must go to print at a certain time. (Therefore, a reporter may give themselves an extra day or two when they tell you what their deadline is in case you are late. For example, if I need to submit my column by Tuesday, I always tell the people I am interviewing my deadline is Monday.) Do note, deadlines are very different for weekly papers and daily papers. As a result, you must send in your press release accordingly.

1. *Weekly Papers:* Send your press release at least a week in advance and a reminder the day before the event, if possible.
2. *Daily Papers:* Send your press release two to three days before the event.

As you imagine, weekly newspapers are different from daily newspapers. The weekly papers are typically short-staffed. They need more time to coordinate the manpower to cover your event. So it is important to get the first press release to the weekly newspapers at least a week in advance, if possible. Do send a reminder a couple of days before the event. (Gauge the manpower, generally speaking, by the number of reporters and the number of stories they cover. If one reporter is covering three or four different stories for one newspaper, there is likely a smaller staff.)

Daily newspapers typically meet in the morning to discuss what will be covered before the newspaper goes to print that evening. A daily newspaper typically goes to bed (to print) anywhere from 6:00 p.m. to midnight. Daily newspapers must go to print at certain times, so their morning meetings around 8:00–9:00 a.m. are essential. Sending a newspaper a press release a day or two in advance is helpful so they can prepare.

Remember that, like TV reporters, newspaper reporters cover different stories as well. You will want to make sure to get in touch with the one who will most likely be interested in covering your story or event.

Radio

Send your press release two to three days in advance.

Much like television stations, radio stations typically meet through-out the day to discuss what will be on-air during the main times of the day: morning, midday, and evening. Depending on the station, sending the first press release a couple of days in advance does not hurt. They will likely want to get a reporter out to your event, but that also depends on the station's manpower. Thus, they must be able to anticipate the staff needed to cover each story. One advantage to radio is that reporting can be done from almost anywhere. Thus, you can essentially act as the reporter and call in from an event. The radio station can listen in and go live from your event. The station can also record you from the event and use your interview for a later show. (If a radio station at first rejects your press release, try again. You can also call the station ten minutes before going into an event and ask if they want live coverage or if they want to chat on the phone immediately after.) Do not be shy. This is where the old adage "the harder you work, the luckier you get" comes into play.

For radio, ask to be on during the 7:30–8:30 a.m. hour. The morning commute to work is chock full of listeners, so you want to specifically request that time slot. Also, be sure to tell the listeners when they need to remember your information. "Yes, you can buy my book. Now for all you drivers out there, now is the time to record this information on your phone. You can buy my book at Barnes and Noble and other major bookstores, or you can go to my website at JillOsborn.com."

Television

Send your press release the day of the event or the day before.

Just like five players from each basketball team must fill the court on the day of a game, producers must fill a show with stories on the day of the show. Hence your story may be used, moved to a certain spot, or cut depending on the news of the day.

The morning crews meet anywhere in the morning from 9:00–10:00 a.m. The afternoon crews meet anywhere from 1:30–3:00 p.m. All of the reporters scour the internet, check emails, or make phone calls prior to the meeting. They are searching for stories. So you want to be sure you send your first press release right before their meeting. You want to be one of the top emails.

If you want a local television station to cover your event on Tuesday, wait until Tuesday morning to the send the press release. Local stations thrive on the fact that they can cover any story, anywhere that day. If you provide information for a good story that day, they will be more eager to cover it, as opposed to writing it on the calendar and trying to remember it, etc. They will have less time to waffle on your story pitch. Instead, the focus is on whether they have enough newsworthy stories, and whether or not yours is linked to one that will be covered. That said, if you have a story that is a slam dunk and you know the news will want to cover it, give them more advance notice.

For a morning or midday show, contact the show as early as possible to book. If you have an event coming up, try to get on the morning or noon show to talk about it prior to the event. The shows will book guests even a year in advance. So it is never too soon to book your spot on the local shows. These guests are hardly ever covering breaking news which is why they can be booked so far in advance. Even offer to fill in during emergency situations, especially on national shows. If a guest cancels or is a no-show, tell the anchor you would like to be the first one on the list to call to help out during a crunch. National shows cover breaking news and have certain guests they know they can go call in the wee hours of the morning to come on the show for a comment. You want to be one of those guests who can go on the show at a moment's notice either by phone or in person.

After every report, make sure your information is on the website and that the receptionist knows your name and number in case listeners or viewers call in for more information.

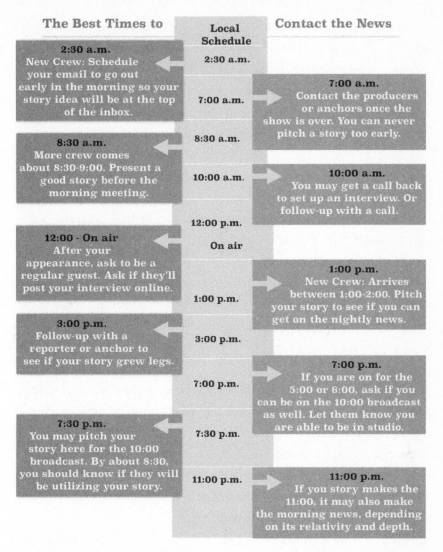

The Best Times to   **Local Schedule**   **Contact the News**

2:30 a.m.
New Crew: Schedule your email to go out early in the morning so your story idea will be at the top of the inbox.

2:30 a.m.

7:00 a.m.

7:00 a.m.
Contact the producers or anchors once the show is over. You can never pitch a story too early.

8:30 a.m.
More crew comes about 8:30-9:00. Present a good story before the morning meeting.

8:30 a.m.

10:00 a.m.

10:00 a.m.
You may get a call back to set up an interview. Or follow-up with a call.

12:00 p.m.

12:00 - On air
After your appearance, ask to be a regular guest. Ask if they'll post your interview online.

On air

1:00 p.m.

1:00 p.m.
New Crew: Arrives between 1:00-2:00. Pitch your story to see if you can get on the nightly news.

3:00 p.m.
Follow-up with a reporter or anchor to see if your story grew legs.

3:00 p.m.

7:00 p.m.

7:00 p.m.
If you are on for the 5:00 or 6:00, ask if you can be on the 10:00 broadcast as well. Let them know you are able to be in studio.

7:30 p.m.
You may pitch your story here for the 10:00 broadcast. By about 8:30, you should know if they will be utilizing your story.

7:30 p.m.

11:00 p.m.

11:00 p.m.
If you story makes the 11:00, it may also make the morning news, depending on its relativity and depth.

Above is a sample schedule for a local television station, when you should contact them, and what you should be anticipating in advance. Feel free to use this information to determine the timing of your press release. Here are further details on what goes on inside a news station:

2:30–3:30 a.m.

New Crew Arrives: Anchors, reporters, and producers come into the station. They take the stories from the 11:00 p.m. newscast and decide which ones are worth implementing in the morning newscast. Here's why this is done: viewers watching at 5:00 a.m. typically were in bed by the time the 10:00 p.m. newscast was on. So the 5:00 a.m. viewers missed stories from the previous night.

The producers, however, want current stories and breaking news. They search for important events that will be happening that day. If you have a story and can schedule your email to go out early in the morning, your story idea will be at the top of their inbox. They may cover your story depending on the news of the day. Be sure to be available for interview. Most morning shows do not have interviews that early, but it is a nice option.

Next, producers write and queue up the videos. The anchors study the material and help write scripts. Reporters are sent to the location of where they will be going live. The show begins to percolate like a cup of coffee, being freshly brewed together.

5:00 a.m.

On-Air. Television and radio shows hit the air waves. The first eight to ten minutes of every broadcast has the most important news known as hard-hitting news. So your story will make a big impact if it runs in those first eight to ten minutes.

Following the first segment is a commercial break. The weather forecast is shown to the viewers, unless it is an important story. Then, it will be shown in the first segment.

After the next commercial break, ensuing stories get fluffier with lighter news. Your story has the potential to be used here. A reporter could interview you as well. For example, if you are holding a food drive and you are trying to drive folks out to your location to donate canned goods, a reporter could be there to help you promote it.

5:30 a.m.

Local stations typically repeat what was seen in the last half hour. This is done because people who watch morning shows are getting ready for work or school. Studies show they watch the news in half hour segments. There is little time to sit down and watch the news like they would in the evenings.

6:00 a.m.
The show repeats the same segments from the 5:30 hour.

6:30 a.m.
The last half hour of the show is typically filled with the most important content from the morning news. You could potentially have your story told multiple times at this point.

6:50 a.m.
Some shows will have a recap of the show's highlights and what is most important for the viewer to know. (You want your story to be aired here.)

7:00 a.m.
Show is over and it is "lunch break" for everyone. Feel free to contact the producers or anchors once the show is over. You can never pitch a story too early to a morning anchor because they have been up since 2:30 a.m. But if you have a new video from that morning, this is a perfect time to try to fit it into the midday show. If you want it to be on the midday newscast, pitch your story to the midday anchor.

Usually a national news cycle starts at 7:00 a.m. because that is when the next set of viewers are awake and tuning in for the first time. It is a key hour for viewers because it is usually when everyone is eating breakfast while tuning into the news. Once again, the first eight to ten minutes of local and national news exposes the most hard-hitting news of the day.

8:00 a.m.
The anchors and producers start producing the midday show around this time.

9:00 a.m.

New Crew Arrives: You want to pitch your story between 8:30 and 9:30 to the dayside reporters. New reporters come in around 9:00 as well as the news director, assistant news director, and dayside producers. At this time, journalists are seeking new ideas to present in the morning meeting. Your goal is to present the reporter with a good story before the gathering.

During the meeting, your story will either be accepted or rejected based upon the news of the day. The 5:00 p.m. newscast is also generally decided upon here. Unless, of course, breaking news pops up. Reporters are required to cover one or two stories a day, depending on the size of the station. Some anchors are required to make a package. (Package: An entire story put together with interviews and a stand-up. Stand-up: Where the reporter talks on camera). The new reporters will be covering stories for the 5:00 p.m. newscast and some possibly for the midday show. Hopefully one of those stories is yours. You should receive a call back after the meeting to set up the details of the interview.

10:00 a.m.

Depending upon how long the meeting lasts, you should be getting a call back to set up an interview. You could also check with the midday anchor or producer to see if any guests canceled last minute. If so, let the anchor know you can fill in.

12:00 p.m.

On-Air. Midday newscast begins. This show does not repeat itself. It airs all new stories the entire hour. After you make a guest appearance, you should pitch the producer or anchor on why you should be a regular guest. Anchors like having regular guests who come on once a month or every couple of months. Then, they do not have to keep searching for as many guests. (One less item to check off their list.) Midday newscasts are more heavy with guests because it is more of a talk show type format.

1:00 p.m.

Show is over. The morning crew meets with the news director to discuss how the shows have gone and review any mistakes. After, the morning crew goes home.

2:00 p.m.

New Crew Arrives: Now would be a good time to pitch your story to the new group of journalists arriving. The evening anchors, producers, and reporters begin their meeting with the news director who fills them in on the stories being covered for the 5:00 p.m. Reporters may or may not be assigned to cover news for the 5:00 p.m. newscast but certainly will cover stories for the 6:00 p.m. and 10:00 p.m. broadcasts. The news is set for the evening.

3:00 p.m.

Now would be a good time to follow up with a reporter or anchor to see if your story grew legs. You should be getting interviewed by now because reporters want to cover their stories before their deadline. Anchors are writing scripts and studying the material for the show. The producers are working on the evening shows with the anchors.

4:00 p.m.

Do not contact the news now, unless you have major last edits or breaking news. The 4:00–5:00 hour is a tense hour because news crews are creating the 5:00 p.m. and 6:00 p.m. newscasts. Thus, the newsroom is a madhouse. Tempers fly. Words are used. Jokes are made for temporary relief from the stress. Make-up is applied and hair is sprayed in preparation for the show. All packages (stories) need to be into the graphics department so any additional changes can be made. Editing bays are all utilized to make final edits to the videos. Videos must be queued up. Final changes must be made to scripts so they can be added into the teleprompter. Anchors and reporters print their scripts. The hum of the live trucks can be heard as they are up and running. The producer or cameraman at the truck holds a phone to an ear. On the other end of the line, a producer sitting in a chair at the station makes sure the reporter knows when to go on-air. Whether the reporter, anchor, producer, or photographer are ready or not, the show must go on.

5:00 p.m.

On-Air. The show is on-air at 5:00 p.m. Once again, the first eight to ten minutes of the broadcast has the most important information of the day. The 5:00 p.m. does not repeat any segments. They have plenty of new stories to fill the necessary air time. Do not contact the news station unless you have updates for the 6:00 p.m. show.

6:00 p.m.

On-Air. The next hour of the show uses some of the 5:00 p.m. content and may have other reporters update you on information presented the last hour. However, it also has some new content. Again, the first eight to ten minutes has the most important news. (The evening viewers are presumably cooking dinner, sitting down to dinner, or on the couch available to watch the stories of the day for longer periods of time.)

7:00 p.m.

If you are on for the 5:00 or 6:00, ask if you can be on the 10:00 broadcast as well. Let them know, you are able to be in studio if need be. Also, ask to have your story on the website.

7:30 p.m.

You may pitch your story here for the 10:00 broadcast. The evening crew is on lunch break. (Or in this case, dinner break.)

8:30 p.m.

By about 8:30 p.m., you should certainly know whether or not they will be utilizing your story. The anchors and producers start producing the 10:00 broadcast.

9:00 p.m.

Only contact the station if you have breaking news or edits to your story. All videos and stories are being finalized during this hour. The 10:00 p.m. newscast is chock full of stories because the evening reporters have video available the early reporters did not. The 10:00 p.m. reporters have video available from the 5:00 p.m. and 6:00 p.m. newscasts. They have new video available from the national news that was shown at 5:00 p.m. and 6:00 p.m. (All local stations can pull video from a national outlet at any time. So an NBC affiliate can pull video from the New York station in the NBC video library. While video is available at any time, the best video is shot throughout the day and evening, so there are more options at night.) Plus, the reporters are able to cover events from that evening, which tend to be more newsworthy. So the reporters have the best packages of the day for the evening newscast (hence, the reason the morning crew who comes in at 3:30 a.m. will use this video in their 5:00 a.m. newscast).

10:00 p.m.

On-Air. The best show is at 10:00 p.m. It has the best video and strongest news of the day. The evening news often has the full attention of their viewers as mothers and fathers wind down from their day. Viewers are sitting on their couch or are in bed fully engrossed in the broadcast.

11:00 p.m.

If you story makes the 10:00 it may also make the morning news, depending on its relativity and depth. If so, ask if you can assist the overnight producer.

You see why it is so important to maintain relationships as well as strategically create a timetable of newsworthy events. Shows want to book guests in advance but are most driven to cover the latest news. Television stations have the equipment to cover breaking news. Radio stations and newspapers try as well, but do not have the manpower a television station does. So radio stations and newspapers must plan ahead. You must, too.

Chapter 7

Going Live in Studio

|f you are invited into the studio to talk about your story, here are some items you need to know before you go. You will typically get more airtime if you are in studio. It is easier for the host interviewing you to have you there in person. It is easier for the cameraman and producers as well. (If you are being interviewed via satellite, there is more communication that must go on between more people, which means more room for error. But of course, satellite interviews happen all the time.)

An Interview That Moves

Before you are live in studio, know that you need an interview that moves. An interview that moves is one in which a camera will move from item to item. It is interactive. An interview that moves provides the anchor with a natural progression through topics. As a former news anchor, I liked the idea of talking about props instead of looking down at my index card for my next question. Plus, I could make new observations and create a more fascinating conversation for the viewers.

Additionally, if you can provide video to back up what you are explaining or bring a prop to demonstrate your idea, you are more likely to get booked on a show. If you notice, when dieticians come on shows, they bring food samples so people can see and hear what is being talked about. Seeing and hearing the information is much more engaging. Plus, viewers retain the information better. You can see why the news likes your story better if your story moves.

An example of this is when Michele and Tarron Coalson of Triad Martial Arts Academy wanted to promote their karate tournament. They were looking to get media attention in order to spread tournament information and to encourage greater participation in the competition. Instead of approaching the news stations and asking them to conduct a regular interview about the price to compete, as well as the location and time, we asked the news if Michele could come on the show and demonstrate some self-defense moves. We offered to bring some karate students in for the demonstration since adults and children would be participating in this family tournament. The tournament would be promoted at the end of the interview. In doing so, viewers would remember the last bit of information seen. It worked.

It was a great interview for the local station for a couple of reasons. First, the interview was interactive. Second, many of its viewers could relate to the subject of learning to defend oneself, even if they may never have done it themselves. We also gave the reporter a sample set of questions and answers (Q&A).

Providing a Q&A Before Your In-Studio Interview

Once a news outlet has accepted your story, send the reporter or anchor covering your story a Q&A sheet. For an anchor, the Q&A is like providing answers to a pop quiz. It not only makes the anchor's job easier, it is your key to guiding the interview. The questions will direct the anchor's focus. You are the expert of the field, so the anchor will likely not fully know the answers to your questions and depend on you to provide the answers.

The Q&A should be informational and informative but not overly complicated. By providing a Q&A prior to the interview, you may be able to anticipate some of the questions. The anchor may use none of the questions, or perhaps all of them. Either way, the anchor will be appreciative he or she does not have to do more research and work, because you are providing a cheat sheet for them. More often than not, anchors will use the Q&A sheet provided.

Knowing the questions—or at least the general approach of the interview—ahead of time will make you more prepared and less likely to freeze up, making the anchor's interview easier. The Q&A sheet we sent for the karate tournament included the name of the guests, along with brief descriptions, so the producer would know the names to put with each guest as they appeared on screen. We also provided a sample introduction that highlighted the message we hoped to convey. Note that we made sure to include pronunciation clues. No one wants to misspeak, least of all a journalist. At the end of the interview, we encouraged the anchor to ask for details about the event in order to remind others to sign up. Here is our sample Q&A:

Guests: Sensei Michele Coalson (karate black belt), Triad
    Martial Arts Academy
Chelsea Crater (23 years old, green belt)
Kattie Holden (10 years old, green belt)

Sample Introduction:
For the first time ever, there will be a karate tournament in Clemmons. Here to show us some self-defense moves and tell us more about the tournament is Sensei (pronounced: sen-say) Michele Coalson.

Sample Question & Answer
1. *One might think of karate as a male-dominated sport, but you are a female black belt who is also a Sensei (Sensei means leader). Did you choose to take karate on your own?*
   Answer: No. My mom initially signed up my brother. He did not want to do it alone. In fact, he eventually quit. I

kept going, became a black belt, and now have my own school where I teach children and adults.

2. *As a female Sensei, do you teach a lot of self-defense classes in addition to karate classes?*

   Answer: Yes. We offer self-defense classes and bully-proof classes at our school and at outside locations. We also emphasize that self-defense is not karate. Our classes focus on preventing and escaping an attack and how to take control of a situation. The need for self-defense has increased dramatically and we tend to play with our cell phones instead of being aware of people and our surroundings in places like college campuses, convenience stores, ATMs, and mall parking lots. These places can be dangerous. Statistics show a rape occurs every six minutes.

3. *Do you have many people who say they don't need self-defense because they carry a gun?*

   Answer: Yes. But realistically, a gun is only going to help you if you see an attacker coming from a distance. In many cases, a gun can fall into the hands of the attacker, making a bad situation even worse.

4. *Are you going to show us some self-defense moves? And who do we have here with us today?* (Demonstration will last approximately 15 seconds.)

   Answer: Yes—today we have twenty-three-year-old Chelsea Crater who has a green belt. We'll demonstrate a self-defense technique today of defending from a choke hold.

5. *Wow—that's impressive. And it looks fairly easy to do. Now, you are also holding the first karate tournament ever to be held in Clemmons, right? Can you tell us about this tournament, Michele?*

   Answer: Yes, this is a big family event. I have three daughters competing. We have fathers and sons. We have a mom and her two children. There are a lot of families participating, adults and their children. We also have a set of triplets participating. There are tournaments held pretty much statewide. For some reason our area—Winston-Salem, Greensboro, and High Point—generally doesn't seem to have many tournaments. We're trying to change that by starting the Triad Open and hoping to build it into an annual event for martial artists in this area.

6. *What events will be at the tournament?*

    Answer: The tournament will feature three events: Kata Forms, which is an imaginary fight, Weapons Kata, and Point Sparring for all ages.

7. *And you have another student here to demonstrate a Kata (cot-ah) Form for us?* (Demonstration will last approximately 30 seconds.)

    Answer: Yes, we have Kattie Holden, another student from our school who is going to show you a Kata called Wansu.

8. *That's impressive. How young or old can you be to start taking martial arts?*

    Answer: Our Little Dragons program starts at age three. But our older students tell us that martial arts help them with flexibility and physical conditioning.

9. *So karate is encouraged for all ages? The Triad Open Karate Tournament is April first at the Old Clemmons Gym and you can register now. If people are interested in finding out more information, where can they go?*

    Answer: You can call us at: (336) 486–6543, go to our website: KIAdvance.net, or like us on Facebook.

After You Are Live in Studio

You should also ask the anchor and producer if the story will be posted on the station's website and if your website can be posted with the story. Hopefully, this will drive more traffic to your website.

Once the interview is over, take a photo with the anchor and post it on your social media page. You can say something similar to, "If you weren't able to catch our interview, we will post it soon. Thanks Lauren for inviting us to the station!" Also, snap a photo with the hair and makeup folks. They can have a thankless job, but they too might post a photo of you on their social media account if you show them kindness and grace.

Then, ask to go into the control room and thank those folks. They are the ones operating the sound, the cameras, and are the producers running the show. Essentially, they are the ones that make you look like a star. You could say something like, "Thank you guys. I know you are the ones who make everyone look good on camera. I appreciate you working hard behind the scenes." You will *instantly* be appreciated by making the extra effort. *People never think to go to the control room.* Get a photo with them as well. Ask if you can take a photo and post it online and vice versa. Then, post a thank you online. For example, "Thank you Joe for mastering the control room during today's interview." In doing so, you are creating a network of allies that few think to cultivate. Finally, be sure the receptionist knows your name and number. If someone decides to call in instead of checking the website, the receptionist will instantly have the information ready for the viewer.

Also ask for a follow-up interview. Let us say, for example, you are a politician and you have just discussed the cuts needed in the proposed budget. After your interview, ask the producer or anchor if they would like to schedule a follow-up interview once the budget is passed to get reaction from the outcome. The news station will accept or reject your idea, but I guarantee you they will appreciate the story idea. Remember what Winston Churchill said: "A politician needs the ability to foretell what is going to happen tomorrow, next week, next month, and next year. And to have the ability afterwards to explain why it didn't happen."

Per Winston Churchill's advice, we tried to foresee the future of each news outlet for the Triad Open Tournament. In order to receive more news coverage, we contacted the local weekly paper at least a week in advance. They are often low on staff and need time to prepare. When the local paper interviewed the Coalsons a week prior to the tournament, it was fresh on the minds of many karate students. The story made the front page of the paper. After the article came out, more people signed up for the tournament because of the article. Michele also began receiving phone call after phone call from people wanting to sign up for her class. When she asked how they heard about her class, they responded, "I read your article." Plus, Michele said there were multiple people in church giving her copies of her article—increasing the number of people spreading her story via word of mouth.

The Coalsons accessed the media and their enrollment rate exploded. Just the small amount of local media exposure provided information and excitement about the sport and tournament. They got more participants in the tournament. They received more students for their year-round class. Next year, the Coalsons can spread the word about the tournament by contacting the journalists and staff members with whom they created rapport. Also, when the Coalsons go to submit the information about the second annual tournament to local schools, they will attach each news story from the first tournament. It will show them as a credible and newsworthy source. Bottom line, the news coverage gave the tournament validation and consequently new karate students. The Coalsons earned money for their business without spending a penny in advertisement.

You can have similar great success with the press. If you use the tips in this book and receive media coverage, please share your success with your friends and with me. Email me, your media expert, at Jills-Media@gmail.com, so I can hear all about your press victories. If your story is not live in studio and is covered by a reporter coming to your event, follow the tips in the next chapter.

Chapter 8

Second Point of Contact: Greet the Reporter

Befriending a reporter at an event not only helps a reporter get what he needs—the truth—it also helps you get what you need. It increases your chances of getting your message in the paper, and it also saves money you might otherwise spend on advertisements. It is a win-win for both sides.

As a prosecutor, Aaron Berlin fought for rights for abused women and provided a voice for women who needed one in the courtroom. Aaron knew how to improve the community. So when he decided to run for district court judge, I was happy to consult with him about ways to increase his media exposure.

The night Aaron approached a journalist, he was at a charity event. Aaron admitted he normally would have sat back and not said a word, but per my advice, he took action. "I did what you told me to," he said. "I introduced myself and asked if the cameraman needed a comment from me. The cameraman said he needed the interview right away and was glad to talk to me because he said he had to race back to the station to put the story together. It worked."

By taking action he got publicity for his campaign while talking about something positive—all with no advertisement cost.

Mahatma Gandhi had a different opinion about the press. He despised them, once saying, "I believe in equality for everyone, except reporters and photographers." Gandhi must have been sensitive about the negative press he received during his career of peaceful protests that enabled India to gain independence from British rule. Whatever the reason, know negative press will happen. There will be reporters who want to report on your fumbles. If you do make a mistake, make sure to tackle it head-on by talking to the reporter with respect. Kindly tell the journalist your side of the story. Take responsibility if need be. Humbleness goes a long way. Do not go into hiding or avoid the press, but do avoid personal attacks online. You do not want to be quoted online for personally responding to one person's post.

To avoid bad press, make sure to always tell the truth. If you lie once, you will never be looked at as a credible source. If you accidentally provide misinformation, correct it immediately. There is no shame in saying, "I made a mistake." But if your mistake goes on air or is printed in a newspaper or online, the mistake grows into a huge problem. So correct it before that happens. Be sure to get back to journalists within a reasonable time. The longer you wait, the closer a deadline looms. Try to befriend journalists on a personal level whenever possible. But do not pester a journalist day in and day out. If your story gets turned down time after time, or you do not get returned emails or phone calls, take the hint. You are doing something wrong. Change your strategy. Know that you can have bad press one week and good the next. The key is to limit the amount of negative exposure.

While reporting at a Donald Trump rally, I met the NBC reporter Katie Tur and complimented her work. She asked me who I was report-ing for. I told her for a paper in North Carolina. I shared how nice I found it to report for the paper because I have three kiddos and the paper allowed me some flexibility. If I was on TV, I would have to be in the office every day. Whereas with the paper, I was able to pick and choose my stories, enabling me to coach my children's sports teams and walk them into their first day of school each year.

"But," I admitted, "I do miss the broadcasting world."

"Yeah," she said with a bit of smile, "I enjoy it, but I have no life right now." She was following Trump from stop to stop during the 2016 presidential campaign. Katie and her crew spent more time traveling and reporting on Trump than Katie spent at home. But that is the kind of life a national reporter leads during a campaign. Whether they like the candidate or not, the reporter must talk about that person day in and day out. The reporter and her crew are always on the road. They are dedicated and hardworking. It is thrilling but tough work with a lot of long hours away from home. You can see Katie worked her tail off. How you can you not respect her work ethic?

When I interned at FOX News, Gretchen Carlson was the same way. Extremely intelligent. Very dedicated to her work. Not only that, she was nice. It did not matter if you were an intern or running for the highest office of our great country, Gretchen treated everyone with the exact same respect. As a result, when I asked her questions about her steps to success, she generously opened up to me.

"I had to make a lot of sacrifices," Gretchen said. "I had to move away from my husband when I was first married because of a job. Just know, to get to national news, it takes a lot of hard work, sacrifices, and is very competitive."

Journalists are just like you. Just like you, a journalist has fought from the ground up. Just like you, a journalist works tirelessly and for long hours for a small amount of gratitude. Just like you, a journalist must conduct many thankless tasks in order to get the job done right. Just like you, a journalist sees the reward is there in the end.

When I first started out as a reporter, I worked for the NBC affiliate news station in Rapid City, South Dakota. The other reporters and I were paid so little, we qualified for food stamps. No joke. It is just the nature of the business when first starting out. Even ordering pizza was quite a luxury at that point. I remember checking every coat pocket and bottom of each purse to scrape together any and all change I had to pay for a hot slice of heaven: pizza. In fact, a news anchor from the other station had to get a side job delivering pizzas. I found this out when she rang my doorbell and delivered a pepperoni pizza to me one evening!

If you go the extra mile for a reporter or photographer—especially if they are just starting out—you will be sincerely appreciated. Become their friend. Just make sure you are a good friend.

> "I've learned that people will forget about what you said, people will forget what you do, but people will never forget how you made them feel."
>
> —Maya Angelou

Cultivating the Relationship with a Reporter in the Field

When greeting the reporter at an event, it is important to follow these rules of reporter engagement:

1. *Greet the Reporter or Persons Covering the Story.* Introduce yourself immediately. As soon as you see a reporter, photographer, producer, etc.—go up right away to greet each individual. Do not hesitate. You are doing this so you can become their ally. You are also notifying the news crew out in the field that you are a source of information and can be interviewed for the story. The sooner the news crew can line up an interview, the sooner they can start shaping their story. Remember, reporters are always on a deadline. They need the story and therefore, they are actively looking for a newsworthy quote. Always have the outlines of a few quotes in your mind, ready to be retrieved smoothly and then tailored to suit the purpose of the moment.

2. *Provide An Information Packet:* Be prepared with a packet of information. In it, include information about the event and a quote from you that is only two to three sentences long. (If it is longer, make sure you note at the end, the quote can only be used in its entirety.) The information will often be used as a reference for the reporter. Here is a great opportunity to tailor the message to the most essential points of your story. Plus, if you cannot talk right away, you are providing him or her with a packet of information that will entice the reporter to interview you. You might say, for instance, "Here's some information for you about today's event. I need to talk to a couple of folks first. Then, we can talk after you scope out the scene. Does that work with your deadline?" This way you are kindly assuring the reporter, they will score the main interview—you.

3. *Guide the Reporter:* Do not leave things up to chance. Inform the reporter who is a good interview and why the reporter needs to talk to which person. For example, let us say Warren is your biggest supporter. You know Warren will talk enthusiastically about you, which in turn, gives you more positive press. It makes sense to suggest to the reporter, "You might want to talk to Warren. He is a veteran who served in Iraq and will tell you why he thinks it is important for more hospitals to provide coverage for all veterans." Guide them to the information you would like covered and the people who are on your team. The reporter will be glad to find a good person to interview. It makes his or her job easier.

4. *Take a Picture:* Take the time to take a photo with reporters with your camera. "Do you want to take a quick photo together?" You can take a picture with your phone and tag them in a post online. Reporters, most likely, will love to tag you in a photo. (If that is the case, why don't they ask?)

Some feel awkward asking for a photo because they want to act as if they are on the same playing field and not be too chummy. However, once you take that photo, you can say, "Will you post that online and tag me in the post?" Do the same thing with the cameraman and any other crew members there. Ask them the same thing about posting it online. Essentially, you are asking each person to promote you, and to some degree, themselves too. Reporters have to be on social media outlets reporting information, especially when out in the field. It is required. So the reporter's social media post might as well be a picture of you. You also need to ask the reporter if the story will be on the station's website and if she will add your website link for more information. This drives more traffic from a highly visited news site to your website.

5. *Nurture the Relationship.* Nurture your personal relationships with reporters. Always follow up an event by going online and thanking the reporter, cameraman, and any other crew members with whom you might have caught a photo with or developed a rapport. It is especially great if you can thank producers. The producers are the ones sitting at the news stations sitting behind their desks. They are hard at work, tapping away at the keyboard, making the phone calls to ensure you are booked on the show, but hardly ever get to meet you. Try to find out which producers you need to thank by asking the reporter which producers are helping with this segment. By thanking all of these folks online, you are publicly writing an online thank-you note. Next, wait for the story to be posted online and post the story on your social media pages. There is no need to write anything in addition to the story. Just post the story all by itself. (That is, unless, of course, the reporter portrays the story in a bad light—no need to post that story!)

6. *Assist the Reporter:* Lastly and perhaps most importantly, just as when you contact a reporter in the news station, you or someone on your team needs to become the reporter's personal assistant. Again, this is a must. You may flinch when you hear "personal assistant," but a relationship between you and the media is critical. Therefore, you must cultivate this relationship accordingly.

How to Assist the Reporter

Here are easy and necessary policies to follow when assisting a reporter:

- *In Newspapers:* Print reporters will be taking photos. Tell them you can provide names for each photo. They will be so thankful you are helping with this because it makes their job a thousand times easier. Plus, they are more likely to print a picture in the paper and post more online if they know the names of each person in the photograph. You will provide them the information needed. Then you will post onto your social media pages whatever is posted on the news site. After the event, if you have extra material, like a speech, hand over those notes. The reporters will appreciate your typed-up notes.
- *On Radio:* Reporters will need to get interviews by microphone. Ask them if you can help find people to interview. Tell them who the people are in the room so they can pick and choose. Also, if there are really great sounds in the room that would help shape the story, point the reporters in that direction. Sound tells the story on the radio.
- *On Television:* As in the case of radio, television reporters will need to put a face with the story and get an interview. So the same principle as above applies. However, another way you can show a little thoughtfulness is to ask

the reporters and photographers if they need help carrying their equipment. They have bulky cameras and few people offer to carry the equipment. Consider also having a white piece of paper for when the reporter or cameraman is setting up the camera. Ask the photographer or reporter if he or she would like to use your piece of paper to white balance (getting the color correct on camera based on the light in the environment). By holding that sheet of white paper, you are making the reporter's job easier. It can be the little things sometimes that make the difference.

When accessing the media, there are so many ways to connect with the newsroom by creating new angles to a typical story. Election season proves to be a prime time to put on the full-court press. If a politician is promising change or promoting a plan of action, perhaps you can refute or defend the proposed policy because you or your business can be an expert on the subject. If so, talk to the news about why the candidate is right or wrong and how you can inform the public of the accuracy of the theory.

Politicians can also increase their access to the media when running either as the incumbent or newcomer to the political arena. There are key factors to get in the news during an election season. Here are some tips you might see as useful:

- *If your opponent is in the paper, you should be in the paper.* A reporter will always try to get a quote from a Republican and a Democrat. If there is a race between three candidates running for judge (a non-affiliated race), a fair reporter should get a quote from all three opponents. If you see a reporter cover a story about your opponent and you have not been quoted, you should call up the station and challenge them to be fair by also adding a quote from you.

- *Give your notes to a reporter after a debate.* A reporter has to keep track of many long-winded answers. Again, if you assist the reporter by providing her with a transcript of your answers, this helps the reporter when noting your answers in her report. Thus, either hand your answers over right after the debate, or tell her you will email your responses as soon as you get home that night. A reporter will be very appreciative for your written responses.
- *If you see a photographer or reporter at the polls, help them.* Remember, if you see a reporter or photographer at the polls during election day, go help them. Tell them the names of people there. Most likely, you know many folks there and they know few, if any. Ask the reporter and photographer where they are headed next and offer advice on who they might want to chat with, if you can.
- *Tell news stations where the after-party will be.* Inform the media of where the after-party will be so the news will be there to cover your celebration. The news wants to cover your emotion whether you win or lose. Notify them in advance of the location. It seems like a trivial reminder, but it is an opportunity not to be forgotten.
- *Don't be afraid of creating controversy.* Creating controversy is an easy way to grab a headline. Go to a Democrat rally if you are a Republican. Go to a Republican rally if you are a Democrat. Notify the reporter you are from the opposite party and are interested in hearing the other side's platform. Offer a quote to the reporter. It is a win-win for you and the reporter. You will be quoted and the reporter will get a quote from a candidate from the opposite party without having to do extra legwork.

When Donald Trump, for example, came to South Carolina, I covered his rally. I noticed there was one attendee the reporters kept interviewing. He was a South Carolina congressman. Why, one might ask, was this one congressman getting so much press coverage? In this case, it was not because he was from the opposing party. He supported Rand Paul, who was still in the presidential race at the time. The congressman talked about all the reasons Trump was in the wrong—whereas everyone else at the rally had the same message about Trump: he'll make America great again. The congressman came with controversy. But here is the irony. Rand Paul lost. Trump won. Guess who works in the White House for Trump? The South Carolina congressman who came with controversy.

The news loves to cover controversy. It is a good show. Stories that come with tension or emotion are the ones the viewers (and voters) will remember. Reporters also love new angles to familiar stories. If you pitch a fascinating story idea with controversy or a different angle, the reporter will want to keep working with you. (Even if the story idea does not pertain to you or your event, pitch it anyway. It is okay to pitch a story that does not pertain directly to you, because then you are observed as a solid news source with additional ideas.) The reporters get what they need: a fresh story. You get what you need: an ally in the news world. Win-win for both.

"If you treat people right, they will treat you right . . . 90 percent of the time."

—Franklin Delano Roosevelt

Chapter 9

Third Point of Contact: You Are the Reporter

A follow-up e-mail immediately after the event that includes video is a good way to get noticed. It doesn't guarantee it will make air, but it increases your chances.
—Jeff Gravley, seven-time Emmy award–winning journalist

As a morning television anchor, I cannot tell you how many times I thought, "This is not a good headline. The only reason we are covering this story is because someone captured it on camera. Boy, did that person luck out because someone had a camera handy." Also, as a newspaper columnist, I cannot tell you how many times I scanned through our newspaper and thought, "The only reason that story made the paper is because someone submitted a photo and we had little news to cover this week. What a slam dunk for that guy who sent in the picture."

You Report

You report on your own event. Your report is your second press release to the newsroom. The second press release is very different from the first because the event has already occurred. It is also your last point of contact with the press and perhaps the most important step. You never know when you will strike gold with your second press release because of how unpredictable the news can be. The second press release is where most people fall short because very few folks seem to know or think about this last step. In fact, many give up on the press once an event occurs. But not you. By providing information to the media about the event, you are informing the station of what the media missed out on and may need to include in tonight's report.

You are now the reporter. What exactly does a reporter capture during an event? It is different for each news medium.

1. A newspaper needs photos from the event.
2. TV needs video, and the radio can use the sound from your video.
3. They all need quotes from the event. Quotes from an expert on the matter and a person affected are typically the best.

You are telling the story. You will need to write out the entire story for the station. What was the event about? What happened? What information was relayed? How were people impacted? Your story does not have to be perfect, but it should be written well enough that the news outlet gets a sense of what the scene was like at the event. You are enticing the news stations with your words. Hopefully, the news will reconsider your story and many do. Better yet, they will use the material you sent them. Therefore, cover the story and send the necessary information: facts, video, photos, interviews according to the media outlet you hope to use. The news may use your information and add your story in the news. Once you have the information, send it *immediately* after the event.

The second press release can be a lot of work and sometimes shows little reward. However, as mentioned before, a lot of the smaller news organizations really appreciate the help. Even if the press showed little interest in your first press release, the second one can yield results. A separate story may have broken that is now relevant to yours. Or a story the station was counting on could fall through. Who is there to provide more news? Your team with a second press release.

Here is an example of a college kid who showed initiative by "being the reporter." He provided a ROSR, or Radio on Scene Report, about a hurricane by going outside with his cellphone and recording the experience. As listeners, we heard the wind gusting in the background. We heard the student describe how gates were being pulled off the hinges, back porch umbrellas were flying down the streets, and each raindrop felt like a smack in the face. The verbal description of the stormy experience was vivid in an auditory way that was great for radio.

NPR news then chose to use his audio recording for their radio broadcast. A reporter called the kid and captured a follow-up interview. The reporter then began to compile her story (called a wrap in the radio world) for the broadcast.

The story went like this: The anchor first introduces the reporter and the face of the story, the college kid. Second, the sound recording gives the flavor of the hurricane's power. Third, facts are presented by the reporter and statistics about the damage caused by the storm. At the end of the story, the reporter uses the follow-up interview to explain the aftermath and asks the young man how he is doing after his first hurricane.

The reporter successfully painted a picture of the person behind the story, captured natural sound (thanks to the student's report), provided statistics about the storm, and then ended with the student's reaction.

Here is what is significant: The video had been filmed first before NPR even knew about this young storm chaser. However, his coverage became very relevant to the latest headlines of that time—the storm. Thus, NPR picked up the video after it had been filmed. The college kid was not an employee of NPR, nor was he pitching a news story. He was just capturing a significant moment in time. Notably, the college student was able to provide NPR news with what they needed *after* the event occurred. At that point, the college student was the reporter covering the storm. He had become the reporter. He shared his story with the news. Just like this young budding reporter, you can share your story with the news and you can share this book with your friends about how to access the media. You are starting to understand exactly what you need to capture for the press.

What to Capture

When you are the reporter, it is important to capture different sounds and visual effects to enhance your story. The next two chapters dive deeper into the needs of each news medium, but here is a general rundown:

- *Sound:* Sound sets the tone of the story. It helps us get a fuller appreciation of what is going on. Hollywood directors know this, which is why music and background soundtracks are used. It is why we hear laughing by an unseen audience in comedy specials. The news is no different in its use of sound from events being covered. In the previous story above, the sound of the whipping wind was very present. You could almost feel the gusts lashing through anyone and anything in its path. While the sound of the video was impactful, also note that sound does not always have to be noise. The sound of silence can also be impactful to film. For example, after a tornado devastates an area and all that is left is destruction—a video of a farmer standing as still as a statue in the sunshine while staring at his house that no longer stands, can be almost more impactful than hearing what he has to say. Perhaps, the next sound you hear is a cow mooing. It stands unharmed but also unfenced. The fence has been uprooted by the tornado, just like the farmer's life.
- *Video:* For TV, you need video as well as sound. We, the viewers, need to hear and see the story in order to feel like

we are a part of the story. Consider also shooting close-up videos as well as wide shots that show us a view of the entire scene. Do shoot video of people's reaction. For example, who doesn't remember the video of the tear-streaked faces of Americans when they learned President Kennedy was shot? The reaction filmed on people's faces was even more impactful after hearing from a police officer who tried to maintain stoicism as he reported on the contents of the case. Fellow American viewers felt that raw emotion as we watched ladies covering up their mouths with both hands in shock and disbelief.

- *Photos:* Photos must relay the same message as on film. Find the emotional impact and capture it on your camera. Always try to include photos of people posing as well as action shots. The photo should be a close-up. No one wants to see dead space. Dead space is the background in the picture like a wall or window that has nothing to do with the significance of the emotion of the picture. Also, make sure to note what was happening in each picture. The editor will need this information for the caption. Make sure to include each person's contact information, professional title, and where they are from. The editor needs this information in order to print the picture. No matter what photo you catch—whether it is a posed photo facing the camera with smiles, two people talking, or a group laughing—try to always capture the emotions displayed on each face.

I've seen photos blown up to take up space in papers because the paper did not have enough news stories to fill each section. Therefore, you should always submit photos to your local and weekly newspapers. A lot of folks do not think about this. Even if you are traveling and are at a significant event out of town, I would still submit photos of the event to the local paper.

Another press-attracting venue can be local philanthropic clubs. We are talking about organizations such as the Rotary Club, the Kiwanis, or the Knights of Columbus. Oftentimes, a lot of folks from these clubs will have a press person who writes up an article for the papers in order to receive the press. It works. The club typically gets media coverage because they submit the necessary information: a written story and photos with information pertaining to the photos. These are often feel-good stories because the events these clubs are hosting are usually for local, worthy causes. Thus, it is of interest to local viewers.

Catching the Emotion

Whether you are gathering sound, video, or photos, the key element is emotion. Again, let us use the example of when President John F. Kennedy was assassinated. The *Chicago Tribune* placed a slew of photos across its front page. There were two headshots side by side. One of John F. Kennedy (JFK) and the other of Vice President Lyndon B. Johnson (LBJ). JFK looks a bit forlorn. LBJ seems to have a small smirk on his face. Below the headshots of the two men: a picture of Jackie Kennedy and a smaller photo of LBJ being sworn into office while standing next to the grief-stricken Jackie who was wearing her bloodstained skirt and jacket. Finally, there is a photo of Lee Harvey Oswald, the presumed assassin. The emotion of the event was caught and the story was told so eloquently through the photos—the tragically young and grave-looking president, the grieving widow, the ambitious vice president who would finally hold the highest office, and the presumed assassin who initiated the entire storm. Lots of emotion in those pictures that the whole country could relate to. The newspaper sold over 1.15 million copies on November 23, 1963, the day after JFK was assassinated.

Perhaps one of the most heartbreaking pictures came from JFK's funeral. It was a picture on the front of the *Daily News*. JFK Jr. saluted his father's casket while surrounded by adults mourning in black.

Credit: Getty Images

If you do not have a photo, use a graphic. In addition to video and photos, graphics or infographics are a visual way to effectively deliver a message. A graphic can help viewers remember your message. The news uses graphics in their newscasts when they do not have video, or need to submit a lot of facts in a creative and visually pleasing manner. In fact, they do it every day. I'm referring to the weather maps, of course. Graphics showing the temperatures for the next five days enable the meteorologist to effectively deliver his message—the forecast. You should consider using graphics, too, when they can help convey the message of your story.

If you are a politician, for example, and saved the city $10,000 with a program you implemented, show the news in an impactful and creative way.

"I saved the city one million pennies. If you stack those pennies one on top of another, it would be a little higher than a stack of 831 six-foot-tall men." Provide a graphic of pennies and a group of tall men next to each other. Get creative. It is okay to get cute with the news. The media is the king of pun.

Gathering Quotes

In addition to providing something for the consumers and voters to see, you must also get reaction from those involved at the event. *You must gather quotes.*

Keep in mind, the way a story is written for a newspaper is different than how it is written for the television or radio. Your quotes can be longer for the newspaper. They can be more in depth. Your words paint the picture. Your keyboard is the paintbrush. Each stroke counts.

In radio, you can also use longer quotes because some of the stories (called packages) can be longer. Sound is your best friend for radio stories.

In television, you must have three or four interviews with folks stating two to three sentences. You'll learn it can be quite challenging to gather information in a two- to three-sentence sound bite. Nonetheless, it is necessary. The station may not use all of them, but it is always better to provide options. Make sure you are one of those interviews. Do not forget to include your short, concise quote. *You do not want them to edit your sound bite. You want them to use it "as is." So you control the message.* This is the time to make every word count. Brevity is your goal. Only the best words that make the best sentences should be used to convey your message. No extra fluff. When you access the media, whether it is in TV, radio, or print, I want to hear all about your success stories. Email me, your media expert, at JillsMedia@gmail.com. I cannot wait to hear from you.

In the meantime, follow along in the next couple of chapters to see what should be included in a second press release for each news medium. First, we will explore the world of print. We observe the art of the newspaper and how you can be in the newspaper each time it is sent to the printer.

Chapter 10

The Newspaper

It's amazing that the amount of news that happens in the world every day always just exactly fits the newspaper.

—Jerry Seinfeld

Newspapers are supposed to present unbiased facts to the public. That said, newspapers' editorial boards also openly support one presidential candidate each election. In my mind, a newspaper is a notoriously powerful source of propaganda. The facts should only be printed. But this is not always the case.

Observe the list of presidential candidates the *New York Times* has endorsed since 1860. Twenty-three of the candidates endorsed were Democrat. Twelve have been Republican. Twenty-five of the forty candidates endorsed since 1860 have won the presidency. Fifteen lost.

However, in 1904 and 1908 the malice that the *Times* had for Mr. Theodore Roosevelt was blatant. The editor of the paper clearly favored anyone other than Roosevelt. In 1904, the *Times* endorsed Democrat Alton B. Parker, calling him, "The antithesis of Roosevelt in temperament and opinion, and quite the equal of the strenuous President in moral courage and political sagacity." Then, in 1908 when endorsing William H. Taft, the *Times* said, "He is less impulsive than Mr. Roosevelt, not given to disturbing utterance, averse to spectacular and ill-judged display." Just imagine the steam coming from Roosevelt's ears. I bet he despised reading that paper throughout the election.

While I will keep the name of the source confidential, I have seen firsthand a politician donate money to a big paper for advertisements and as a result receive only positive press—not a single negative story about that representative. Newspapers are influenced.

Some argue the newspaper will eventually be put to rest because of the digital world. But as my eighth-grade English teacher, Mr. Michael Rewald, always said, "The kindest and cruelest part of life is the necessary element of change." In my opinion, the newspaper will continue to adapt. No matter what the technological world invents or reinvents, a person will always want to have a paper to physically hold in the hands.

Most of those reading are older adults. Recognize that when considering your audience and to whom you want to aim your message. Do not neglect those readers—*greater proportions of older folks vote more than any other age demographic and spread important information via word of mouth.* Be smart. Court them through good, old-fashioned newsprint media. They may be some of your most ardent fans and fervent Americans. Also, remember, these ladies and gents grew up in a time when your word was your bond. If you can get them to recommend you to a friend, that endorsement is irreplaceable.

Provide These to Get in the Paper

1. *Photos.* You guessed it. You can never provide enough photos. (However, if you can provide video as well, your press release will gain superior strength. The video may be displayed on the paper's website, further increasing your press.) If you have great photos, try to make sure they are of high quality (although it is still better to provide some pictures than no pictures at all). Also, be sure to submit them as early as possible. Do you remember how newspapers are on a strict schedule? You can have the most amazing photo in the world, but if it is not submitted by the paper's deadline, your photo will not be printed.

However, if you submit the photo in time, it can be really effective. Photos, for example, proved to have an impact during the Civil War, the first war well-documented with pictures. Interestingly, even then the photographic reports were being manipulated. It seems the photographers would stage the pictures before they shot them. The photographers would move the bodies into groups or piles to exaggerate the slaughter.

2. *Information from the event.* Include where it was held, when, and the purpose of the event.
3. *Quotes.* Gather quotes from two to three sources with about five to six sentences in length. Ask the sources to describe their thoughts about the event.

The Importance of a Headline

You know how real estate is all about location, location, location? Your story is all about headline, headline, headline. Some argue the headline of your story is more important than the story itself. Why is that? *Too many times people glance at the headline of the story and believe they now know the full story.* As a result, you must make sure the headline is more than accurate and favors your message. It would not hurt to suggest a couple of headlines for the reporter or editor, so they know exactly what the story should portray.

Let us say, for example, your story is about how important it is for a newspaper to utilize photos. The headline could be: "A Photo Is Worth 1,000 Words or More!" Consider how the exact same story could have a negative connotation by changing the headline: "Do Photos Really Tell the Truth?"

Perhaps one of the most famously erroneous headlines occurred on November 3, 1948. The *Chicago Daily Tribune* wrote on the front page, "Dewey Defeats Truman." Obviously, Harry Truman won the presidential seat and defeated Thomas Dewey. The paper wrongly anticipated too early that Dewey would win and submitted the paper to go to print. The headline was dead wrong, but it was too late. The next morning, Truman held up the paper with a gigantic smile.

The wrong headline had turned into a photo opportunity for the newly-elected president. Truman's photo, holding the paper, was just as impactful as the wrong headline.

Credit: Getty Images

Daily Newspapers

Each morning, the folks at the papers have their daily meetings to decide which stories are important to cover. Reporters will pitch stories, while the editors will have the final say on which stories are covered. One guiding factor for the editors is how much space is needed to fill in the newspaper. This is known as the "news hole." The news hole refers to how much space is left after advertisements have been completed, and is noted during each morning meeting. (Of course, the paper will always make room for advertisements because that is how they make their income in addition to the subscriptions.)

Longer stories or features are pitched by reporters at the meetings but news that needs to be covered that day are assigned. Editorials and feature stories can be done days in advance or written that day by editors to fill the news hole. (So when you see features in a Sunday addition—which is always the whopper of that week's papers—those stories have been written and edited many days prior to the paper going to bed.)

The reporters come back with their stories. They are written, edited by editors, and graphics and/or photos are added. Once all the stories are in, the front page—which is the most important page, and usually has the most up-to-date information—is finalized.

When a newspaper is finally completed with every photo, graphic, and headline in its perfect place, a paper is ready to go to print. Daily newspapers are put to bed anywhere from 6:00 p.m. to midnight depending on the paper. So deadlines are extremely important to the newspaper reporter. The sooner you can get them information, the better.

Daily newspapers want to report on the majority of political stories or consumer tips but may not have the man power, unless, of course, the paper is based in one of the big cities like Chicago, Boston, Washington, DC, etc. Those papers will have more employees. But the ones in the smaller cities spread throughout the rest of the United States need assistance. You can get some space in the newspapers by actively engaging with the papers and strategically providing each with the information they need: numerous photos, longer quotes from two to three sources, and a breakdown of what happened at the event.

Weekly Newspapers

Remember, the weekly newspapers are the little guys. In some ways, they best reflect the community because they have a good read on what is going on with the local leaders, law enforcement, shop owners, waitresses at the local coffee shop—you get the idea. Their stories can seem more personal, and have the potential for a regular Joe or Joan in the community to relate to them. They will more likely know the unfortunate fellow cited for DUI or the youth whose picture is in the paper for making Eagle Scout. Their resources are likely to be considerably less than the daily papers. And although their readership may be smaller, it is likely to be a very loyal crowd. Like the daily papers of the bigger cities, their readers are older. They read the paper because they are very interested in the goings-on in their community. It is also a great place for feel-good stories—atta-boys, if you will, for the people who are doing good things in their community.

Weekly newspapers are put to bed the same day each week. Here's a sample schedule:

- **Monday:** Stories and advertisements are due on Monday, so they can be finalized on Tuesday.
- **Tuesday:** Tuesday is the busiest day because it the last day to collect all the information before the paper is put to bed. The paper will likely go to bed anywhere from 3:00 to 5:00 on Tuesday.
- **Wednesday:** The paper will be available at 8:30 a.m. in local stands on Wednesday.
- **Thursday:** The paper is delivered to mailboxes on Thursday.
- **Following Week:** Many newspapers will put the stories on the paper's website a week later. They deliberately wait to put the stories online in hopes that folks will buy the newspaper first. The other option, is to not allow for the entire story to be read online and charge folks for a digital subscription. The bigger papers tend to use this policy of digital subscriptions. After all, they won't stay in business for long if they write for free!

If you have a great story you want to get out to the community, call the weekly newspapers. Better yet, walk in and say, "Hello, I'm, Jill. I just wanted to introduce myself. I may have a story that would be of interest to you." They will likely be a tight-knit little group, but easy to talk to because they are interested in what is going on if it is newsworthy. Weekly papers are always looking for stories and typically have few people to cover it. So if you walk in, someone may be able to cover your story right then and there.

The weekly newspapers would love to report on political or professional events. While small newspapers certainly do not have the manpower, they do want your newsworthy stories. (The same goes for online papers both daily and weekly.) So if the paper cannot cover your story themselves, always offer to take pictures and submit them to the paper.

The bottom line here is, subscribers of the weekly newspaper are loyal readers and usually community-oriented. The readers believe being informed about their local community is important. Friends, family, and grandchildren have likely made an appearance in the paper at one point or another. It can be a positive, low-pressure way to bring attention to your event or to convey a message to a smaller community. As the Huffington Post states, people in the community believe most media outlets have low morals. But, neighbors believe in the news outlets they rely on regularly.

> "As an example, only 24 percent of Americans say they believe the news media in general are "moral." But that number more than doubles, to a majority of 53 percent, when people are asked about the news media they use most often."
>
> —*Huffington Post*

Op-Eds and Letters to the Editor

1. *Op-Eds*, essays published opposite the editorial page are not my favorite form of messaging. People may not read the entire piece. Plus, op-eds may appear a bit biased. It is, after all, an opinion. People who are in the news do not need to write an op-ed because they are sought out by reporters. While op-eds can be a place to speak about your line of thinking on an issue, there are other, more beneficial ways to find a way to convey your message. Having said that, op-eds can be a great place for businesses to get some name recognition, especially if it is in a national paper.

2. *Letters to the Editor* are a good way to garner support around your cause. The key is to have others write the letter to the editor about you or your product. It just makes for a better testimony coming from someone else. In our day and age in which people are use to sound bites, it is important to remember not be too wordy; five to ten sentences should convey the message easily. Contemplate using bullet points. People may not always remember your message, but they can retain bullet points. Do remember, however, the point of the letter is to be a public testimonial for you or your product.

I want to emphasize one final time: if you want the newspaper to report your story well, provide photos. Photos tell your story. Capture candid pictures of people and their faces reacting to the emotion of the event. Candid pictures are the best but staged photos should be included as well. However, if you also want to access the news stations and receive coverage on TV, you will need to submit a video. A video makes a tremendous difference no matter which media outlet you will access.

Chapter 11

How to Record for TV and Radio

F OX Sports actually encouraged their viewers to become reporters during NASCAR season. On their website, the network had an article about how to become a reporter for the Daytona 500, how to properly shoot video, where to submit it, and so on. One of the headlines of their story said, "Video Orientation: Wanna make the show? Shoot it properly." They went on to explain the importance of holding a cell phone horizontally with the picture below.

Credit: FOX Sports

Always make sure to turn your cell phone horizontal when filming a person or event. If you look at a TV or computer, they are all shaped like a boxcar on a train track. Therefore, you must film accordingly so the news can use your video to fit the horizontal shape of your TV and computer.

Here is a more serious example of when a cell phone video was used by the news. When Gretchen Carlson was suing Roger Ailes for sexual harassment, her story was everywhere. Each news outlet and social media site was talking about the former FOX anchor suing her former boss. As one can imagine, controversy swam around the big story like sharks around its prey. Roger Ailes had created FOX, the top cable news network. Carlson was making a big accusation against a top dog. So story after story was popping up like popcorn kernels in a steaming pot.

Most likely, Carlson and Ailes were advised by their lawyers to keep quiet about the details of the case. Roger Ailes diligently stayed silent. However, Carlson responded to the news stories with a simple cell phone video of herself talking to the camera in a white jacket.

Her statement: "Hi everyone, I want to support all women who have been victims of sexual harassment. It's time for us to come out of the shadows and let our voices be heard because it is so important that we will not be silenced."

Why was Carlson's response so effective?

1. *Video:* By providing video, all news mediums picked up Carlson's video clip and used it in their broadcast, online, on the radio, and in print. Why? Because Carlson provided a new dimension to the Ailes/Carlson lawsuit—a video comment. In it, she looked confident, compassionate, and sure of her message.
2. *Timing:* Her video was posted during the workweek— which is usually when most people watch the news: Monday through Friday. (If you have bad news, release it on a Friday night. That's when it is most likely to be overlooked and by Monday when news coverage resumes, your bad story has become old, stale news.)
3. *Length:* Her video was eleven seconds long with only two sentences. If she would have provided an entire paragraph, reporters and producers would have sifted through the video, deciphering which quote they deemed worthy. However, Carlson chose the quote. She did so by only

providing a short and precise comment. Never give the press too much material. You want them to quote your narrowly-focused message. Too much content means too much out-of-context quoting. Carlson was able to send out a focused message about the true contents of the case: fighting sexual harassment and paving the way for future victims. On that day, Carlson was in the driver's seat.

Carlson settled the lawsuit with Ailes before it went to court. Carlson won $20 million and has since been named one of the most influential people in the world by *Time* magazine. The former FOX News journalist is now making sure other victims do not suffer as she did.

Behind the Scenes: TV

There are two times when breaking news may slow down on TV:

1. *The weekends.* The varsity team covers the news during the week. The junior varsity team covers the news on the weekend, except for sports, occasionally. Big games can bring in the important sports anchors.

2. *The summers.* Summers tend to be slower because more folks are on vacation. Therefore, if you are trying to receive press on someone's show and you want to get your foot in the door, pitch your story to the weekend crew or during the summer when the TV stations are more receptive to new sources and stories.

Do note, Sundays tend to have high ratings. Sunday's national shows wrap up the main events from last week's news, while also highlighting next week's upcoming events. Most local shows are on-air in the evening. They too have a high number of viewers because they also provide a sneak peek into the week ahead.

Video Quote

As mentioned previously, make sure that whatever you write or say will convey your message in one single, impactful quote, so that your words cannot be taken out of context. Look at Martin Luther King Jr.'s speech, "I Have a Dream." The speech was given at the March on Washington for Jobs and Freedom on August 28, 1963. If you say, "I have a dream," everyone thinks of King's speech. His quote is still remembered, decades later.

To send an impactful quote for TV, quotes need to be short and concise, just like Martin Luther King. If you are giving a speech, being repetitive in a distinct message can also be effective. Ideally, your clear, concise sentences will convey your message in two to three sentences just like the ones Gretchen Carlson executed. If the reporter wants more, they will ask. By using shorter quotes, you control the message. You control the content. (Quotes can be longer for radio. But I would advise you tell the station to use all of the quote or none at all. However, if you are under a time crunch and need to send a video quote to both a TV station and radio station, I recommend the more concise video quote.)

Here is why it needs to be a video quote: The news needs to know you can speak intelligently on camera. They need to know you will not freeze the moment camera begins recording as a microphone is catching your every tone and tenor. Plus, a video quote is more entertaining than a black-and-white press release. One study sponsored by Xerox showed that color increases readers' attention spans and recall by 82 percent.

What Not to Do

Businesses that want to promote an event will talk about the times of the event and how much it costs to participate. While the information is important to the business owner because they want all the participants to know how much money to bring and where, that information will not fuel the excitement of a journalist. The journalist is excited about: how many viewers will be impacted by the event and if someone will talk on camera about the personal effects from the event.

A common mistake politicians or their communication directors make is submitting boring videos via press release. An easy video to send is of a politician speaking on the House or Senate floor recorded on C-SPAN. The last time C-SPAN was entertaining was when former FBI director James Comey testified about his secret memos kept after conversations with President Trump. If you are not the former FBI director, then do not submit your C-SPAN video to the news. Journalists want to see politicians interacting with others. The viewers want to see some action. The news directors understand that and will provide the viewers only with what they want to see. Therefore, if your video is boring, it will not be used. Your video does not need to be shot like a Steven Spielberg movie. There are ways to entice the news through various types of simple video techniques easy to capture with a cell phone.

Video for Local News

As in any line of business, there is a certain vernacular used by news stations. The more news terminology you understand, the better you will be able to communicate with a journalist. Here are some terms you need to know and the importance of understanding them.

- **VO:** Video of the event.
- **B-Roll:** Video of the event. People in the news industry may ask if you have any extra B-Roll of the event. They are essentially asking if you have any extra video of the event.
- **SOT:** Sound on tape or, simply put, an interview. Remember, the two types of people featured in SOTs are experts (CEOs, lawyers, coaches, etc.) and the man on the street (a consumer, voter, sports fan, etc.)
- **VO/SOT:** Video/Sound on Tape. (VO/SOT is pronounced: *voe-sought*.) Local TV and radio stations are always looking for a VO/SOT. The reason being, any anchor can use

the video and interview in their broadcast. Video about the story is useful, but an interview adds dimension to the story.

- **Package:** A package is the story the reporter puts together. The segment is typically two minutes long. In the package, the reporter will have various interviews throughout. The reporter's voice will be heard in the background explaining the events of the story. The reporter will also do a stand-up in the middle of the package. That is where the reporter talks directly into the camera. In the package, the reporter is encouraged to use creativity, sound, interviews, and video to tell the story.
- **Live Shot:** In a live shot, the reporter usually stands in one place while presenting the story to the anchor. However, good reporters will move in a live shot, creating a more entertaining form of presenting the story.
- **Hit Time:** The time you go on air.
- **Chyron:** The label at the bottom of the screen during an interview. (Chyron is pronounced *kie-ron*. The beginning part of the word rhymes with "lie.") For example, if I was the one being interviewed, the chyron might read, "Jill Osborn—Author: *Accessing the Media.*"

Remember to include yourself when you send in a video quote. Nonetheless, to increase your chances of getting on the news, you can also use man-on-the-street footage. By putting a face with the story, you are creating relatable emotion that will be left with the viewer once the story is over. In some cases, you can serve as the MOS, if your raw emotion uncovers a touching story.

If you have ever seen *Undercover Boss,* you will understand what I mean by the MOS carrying the emotion of the story. In that television show, the boss dresses up in a disguise to work as a new employee. The boss appears to be the main character of the show, but he always finds another employee to help him. Almost every time, the employee ends up stealing the spotlight of the show. When you see the emotion of the employee after she finds out the person she has been assisting is the boss of the company, the shock is real and entertaining. Once the boss says he will also be giving her financial compensation such as a pay-raise and scholarship money for a college education, the employee is overcome with happiness and tears of joy. Her emotion is raw. The average person can relate to her gratitude and relief to be getting a break from the School of Hard Knocks.

Here is another example. Tony Golding, the owner of Golding Farms, is known as the king of condiments in the South. He sells items like honey, steak sauce, and salad dressings to stores like Walmart, Lowe's, and many others. Of course, Golding has buildings full of employees. However, one specific staff member is a chaplain. Like Coca-Cola, Golding hired a chaplain full-time to allow his employees to pray at work. It was a good news story. But that was not all of it. The chaplain was not only a great MOS, but he had an unbelievable story to tell.

The chaplain's daughter was a walking miracle. She was born with epilepsy and had grand mal seizures—the worst kind possible. The doctor said she would be lucky to live to be a young adult. But on a mission trip in Chile to help rebuild a church, the chaplain and his wife were offered a new drug to alleviate seizures. The drug had not yet been approved by the FDA. The couple gave their daughter the drug anyway. After not talking for months and being strapped to a wheelchair due to the thrashing of the dangerous seizures, the girl woke up the next day and asked her parents what they were going to have for breakfast.

"My wife and I still say those are the most beautiful words to this day," says Chaplain Denny St. Clair.

As you can see, these stories evoke emotions. You can be similarly engaging by thinking of these questions when being interviewed:

- Why is my story important?
- Why am I holding this event or supplying this information?

- How can I explain the soul of the story in two or three sentences?

The need to be precise reminds me of one of my favorite quotes about the difficulty of writing concisely. It was in a letter from the great seventeenth-century mathematician Blaise Pascal to one of his friends. He said, "I would have written a shorter letter, but I did not have the time." Still, you will have remarkable results if you can make brevity one of your top priorities. When you do have that worthwhile news moment, email me, your media expert, at JillsMedia@gmail.com. You can share what you learned with me or talk about it with your friends to let them in on our secrets of accessing the media. Either way, I am excited to hear about your good fortune.

Video for National News

National news always wants B-Roll. Your B-Roll is the extra video of the event or story. News stations will take video from their own video library, shoot new video, or take video from other stations within the same affiliate. The very last option is to take video from other news outlets and credit that source (which is not something a news outlet wants to do because that would mean the other station is getting free advertisement as being the leading source.)

An example of national news using video from a local affiliate came when a large group of violent protesters basically shut down the city of Charlotte, North Carolina. The national NBC News station initially used video from the Charlotte NBC affiliate because they were on the scene immediately. A national correspondent and photographer were then sent down from New York to cover the event and capture the latest video and interviews. Many other national and local stations followed the same style.

Each segment for a national news show has to have a certain amount of footage or video. A lot of national stations will use their own B-Roll while interviewing you on camera in a side-by-side shot. In an interview on FOX, I was one of three guests on the female power panel. One of the headlines of the day we discussed was about Pope Francis. While I discussed the impact of his personality and power, video of the pope was shown beside me on screen. Notice, in this case, I am the source of expert and the B-Roll is of the pope.

Jill Osborn:
Subject Matter Expert

Pope Francis:
B-Roll to explain what Jill is saying

Here is an insider tip. If you provide the B-Roll, you are assisting the producer and adding fresh content to their news show—which is very appreciated by the producers. More content will make the story more entertaining, and you are more likely to air for a longer period of time.

Very few people think to provide B-Roll, so doing that will give you an advantage. You can film extra footage of you or your brand. While it may not work every time, it is certainly worth a shot. If you are trying to pass a bill about ways to enhance health care for veterans, for example, the national news may start with video of veterans. But you can also provide them with video of:

- you talking to veterans
- you at your desk writing/talking on the phone
- you walking to the House/Senate floor to speak
- you talking with other representatives on the floor
- you voting on the floor

If you're a business rolling out a new product, or if you need to get the word out about a program, you could film:

- you working on the new product
- you talking to others about the product
- close-ups shots of the products or advantages the consumer will gain
- people buying the product

When filming product shots, have your company's name or logo on the product or in the background.

Providing this kind of B-Roll has several benefits. The news outlet now has more footage at their fingertips. It is one less job for the producer. Plus, the video is up-to-date. You are passing along recent and relative video all while branding you or your company as you receive what is akin to free publicity from a credible source.

The Secret to Really Great Video

Sound is the key to great video. Imagine a basketball game. It is the last three seconds. The point guard shoots. You hear the sound of the buzzer, see the shot go in, and hear the roar of the crowd. The sound of the buzzer and the roar of the crowd are very dramatic. If you just saw the clock count down the last three seconds and the shot go in, the video would not be as exciting.

Ever listen to the news on the radio? You listen to the reporter, but do you ever listen to the extra sound inserted into the story? Ever hear the shuffling of the papers while the anchor reads the news? The anchor is doing this to signal you, the listener, a new story will be read. Consider this example of enticing listeners through sound: One time I heard the radio teasing a story coming up after the break. (A tease is a short blurb used to try to get listeners to stay tuned for the next story.) On the radio station I was listening to, three people read the tease—each reading a sentence—to entice listeners. The change in pitch and pattern of each voice made me listen more intently to the tease of the upcoming story. No question, sound invites a listener on radio and on TV.

Your cell phone can capture great video. To get great sound, consider using separate microphones to attach to the phone. Film as much sound as possible. But make sure each video you film is only about five seconds long. Be sure to film the extra background noise. The background noise is called natural sound, also known as NAT sound. If you are a politician, for example, who introduced a bill that would allow the blend of ethanol into a gasoline's supply, I might film this at a gas station to really get some great NAT sound and video. Some ideas to think about:

1. A close-up of the gas station sign as the sound of cars whiz by in the background. (All four corners of the gas station sign fill the entire screen of the camera while the sound of the cars creates great NAT sound.)
2. A wide-shot of the politician pulling out the gas handle. (Take four steps back from the politician and then film him or her, essentially from the knees up.)
3. A close-up of the gas nozzle clicking into the gas tank. (Great NAT sound.)

4. A wide-shot of the politician opening the door to the gas station as the bell rings above the door to notify the gas station attendant a customer is there. (Great NAT sound and helping the story move along by notifying the viewer about the sequence of events.)
5. A close-up of the cash register as it rings to check out the politician. (Great NAT sound.)
6. A wide-shot of the politician collecting his change.
7. A close-up of the politician leaving the store as the door dings again. (Great NAT sound.)
8. A close-up of the gas tank being closed on the car. (Great NAT sound.)
9. A wide-shot of the politician getting into the car. (Signaling the story is almost over.)
10. A close-up of the seatbelt clicking into place. (Great NAT sound.)
11. A video quote from you.
12. A video quote from an MOS (man on the street).

Now you have video and an interview. You have various shots that are about five to ten seconds long. Clips used on the news are usually about three seconds. So there is never any need to film one item for fifteen seconds or more. By providing various short and concise clips, the news station has what it needs without a reporter ever setting up a camera. You can send each clip separately to the news station so the reporter or anchor can pick and choose which video is needed. You might also put the clips together on YouTube or on your cell phone. Cell phones now have iMovie or "Memories" where you can put your clips together easily with music. Adobe has a free app for Android devices. However, do not become complacent and just count on these applications. Search the internet for the latest trend to make a movie on your phone. The latest trend will be the easiest way to put your clips together because the tech guys want to keep it super easy for the consumer.

All video compilations must be two minutes or less. A package cannot be longer than two minutes. Again, brevity is your friend. Unless you are providing extra B-Roll to a station, keep it short. The reason stories should only be two minutes is in direct correlation to a person's attention span. The two-minute rule is also true for the internet. The first item a person sees in an online video is the picture. The second, the title. After that, they check how long it is. Typically, if a video is two minutes or less, they will engage in the video. If it is longer, they will not watch it and are on to their next task.

You might also keep in mind that we do not want folks to get bored or desensitized to your videos. Therefore, rotate the news stations to whom you send the video. The same news station will not want to show you every week anyway. Be selective for each story. Track these submissions with a chart that notes who used your video, who did not, and on what date.

Even if you create a phenomenal video, the news may choose not to use the content. Do not fret. There are ways to utilize it. Use a creative or catchy title and post the video to your website or social media pages to drive people to your page. Websites with videos receive the most traffic.

How to Warm Up the Tongue

Reporters or anchors will use these practice tips to prepare before they go on camera. It is a useful tool to make sure your message sounds crisp. You will want to talk with confidence and clarity. It is important to enunciate and practice these techniques because what you practice in private, you will perform in public. Here are some practice tips to help you sound exceptional on camera, which will increase the quality of your video as well.

1. Before shooting a video, practice what you are going to say first. Write it down or jot down bullet points.

2. Next, warm up your tongue. You can do this by saying each sentence with a pencil laying horizontally in your mouth. It strengthens your tongue and helps you enunciate. (Actor Jim Parsons on the hit show *The Big Bang Theory* said he used the pencil trick while practicing his script of long-winded scientific terms.)

3. You may also practice tongue twisters. (Two of my favorite tongue twisters to repeat quickly three times: "Red leather, yellow leather." And: "Six small slick seals." Also, the book *Fox in Socks* by Dr. Seuss is a phenomenal book to read aloud to warm up your voice and tongue.)

4. Always sit up or stand up straight. Then, roll your shoulders back. (Do news anchors slouch? Hardly ever. In fact, many have pillows behind their lower lumbar to help support the "L" shape the body makes when sitting properly at the anchor's desk.) Sitting or standing up straight provides a nonverbal air of confidence and knowledge of the subject matter. Hence, your body language will convince viewers of your confidence in yourself and in your message.

5. Connect with the camera. Smile. Act as if the lense of the camera is your best friend.

6. Be yourself and have fun. Everyone loves watching a charismatic person. Look at Ronald Reagan, for example. The former president had some of the biggest responsibilities of any American, but all the while he seemed confident and even joyful at times. It was reassuring.

Once you accomplish these tasks, you will be ready to post your videos and news stories on your social media sites.

Chapter 12

Social Media

eMarketer projects that mobile ad spending will account for $45.95 billion this year and that by 2019 it will cover one-third of total ad costs in the U.S.

—Forbes

If your social media pages and website were a cup of coffee, how full would it be? Are you maximizing your potential and filling your cup to the brim to entice voters and clients? Hopefully, you are utilizing this outlet. Social media statistics according to the company Brandwatch:

- The internet has 3.5 billion users and the number continues to grow.
- Ninety-one percent of retail brands use two or more social media channels.
- Internet users have an average of 5.54 social media accounts.
- One million new active mobile social users are added every day. That's twelve each second.
- There are 1.65 billion active mobile social accounts globally and these number continue to increase.

Voters feel disconnected from Washington. Consumers are sick of talking to a robot telling them to Press 1 for English and 2 for Spanish.

Social media and the news, nevertheless, gives them some hope of feeling connected—at least on a technological level.

Everything needs to be on social media these days. You never know, however, who is going to be getting their information from the news outlets, online, or both. All news mediums recognize the importance of having an online presence. Therefore, they try to increase their online presence by posting stories as much as possible and on as many avenues as possible. The website is constantly updated. Producers are constantly updating their social media pages while at their desk. Reporters are required to post information that is breaking while they are out in the field. Anchors are required to update their viewers online and engage them with questions.

"According to a new study by computer scientists at Columbia University and the French National Institute, 59 percent of links shared on social media have never actually been clicked: In other words, most people appear to retweet news without ever reading it."

—*The Washington Post*

Get More Press Coverage Online

Do not expect a reporter to post your story online. It is your job to ask the reporter or anchor to post a preview of your story on their social media pages so that you can re-post. You can even do that with the producers or photographers. Take pictures with each person and post the photo. Thank them for their contributions in the post. You want to make sure you ask who is working on your segment and give credit to all of them. There are a lot of people behind the scenes who truly do not get credit for a lot of hard work. Ever. What you are doing is teasing your message so folks will know there is exciting news to anticipate.

By doing this, you build curiosity and draw more attention, while also complimenting those involved.

> "By clicking on a 'thumbs up' or 'thumbs down' icon, constituents can give politicians an instant read on opinions and positions posted on their Web pages, sort of a rudimentary straw poll that is faster, cheaper—but less accurate—than a high-priced telephone poll."
>
> —*U.S. News & World Report*

Get Your Website on the News Station's Website

- Once the story is complete, ask the journalist or producer to post the final story on their social media pages or the station's website. The more the journalists' and stations' websites post your story, the better the opportunities for your story to explode and impact more viewers.
- Ask if you can put your website at the end of the story for viewers to learn more information. Here's why: a lot of times, at the end of news stories, you may notice a paper will write, "For more information about how you can contribute to the Food Bank, go to www.FoodBank.com." TV anchors might also say on the news, "If you have any information about this robbery, please call Crime Stoppers at (212) 555–1212."

When you ask a reporter or producer directly, you could say, for example, "And would you mind adding my website at the end of the story so folks can receive more information? I can send you the direct link if you would like." Obviously, anytime you can have another journalist post your website on her site, you are tapping into more people that you may not have reached through your own site. Asking this simple question offers an easy opportunity to drive more traffic to your site.

> "A majority of U.S. adults—62%—get news on social media, and 18% do so often, according to a new survey by Pew Research Center, conducted in association with the John S. and James L. Knight Foundation."
>
> —Pew Research Center

What Not to Do

Do not be wordy. Better yet, say nothing. When posting the news link to your social media pages, use zero words. The writers for news stations are excellent at creating catchy headlines and having flashy photos. They write these every day and have more practice than you. Therefore, when you copy the link from the news station and post it onto your site, let the story speak for itself. Write very little or nothing at all. Too many times people give away the entire story in a sentence or two. There is no cliffhanger to entice the viewers.

For example: Often times, I have seen folks write, "Had a great time interviewing with news station ABCD. We talked about jobs. They are on the rise."

Okay. Jobs are on the rise. The secret is out. Consequently, people probably won't click on your link. However, if you want to entice your audience, write something like this: "Jobs: On the rise or going down the gutter?"

Using a Photo to Entice

When you tease your message, use an image. Remember, images remain constant in someone's mind. Images are more impactful than words. A picture will cajole viewers into clicking the "Play" button so they can further investigate what the buzz is about. We want the average Joe to know the full story. Not half of it. In order to know the full story, that person must click on your link. When the viewer clicks on your link, he or she will learn jobs are on the rise—and you are seen as contributing to the job increase in some form or another because you are a part of this news story.

The following is another example of the power of using images. Let us say you are making a video or commercial with a very strategic message the public needs to hear. You have had it professionally made and you really want it to grow some legs and take off. What should you do to tease the video or commercial before it is released? Time it out to perfection by using a strong tease. So once all the tape is off the editing floor and ready to go online, email all of your contacts and notify them you will be giving them a sneak peek of what you will be posting online, or the commercial that will soon air on TV. You want them to feel like they are getting inside access.

You can also post a picture of a video camera and this caption on your social media pages: "Just wrapped up a video shoot. Stay tuned—I will post the video Tuesday." Folks by nature will be curious about the words "Video Shoot." The simple words will pique interest and the photo confirms the desire to see and know more.

In approaching it this way, we are getting people excited about the video. It is much like the folks in Hollywood and how they tease viewers with movie trailers. The goal here is getting people to think: "Video camera. Film. Watch the Senator's film."

A prosecutor, Aaron Berlin, made a video for his campaign while running for district court judge. He asked me to give a testimonial in the video and I agreed. After we wrapped the session, I advised him on the importance of the title of his video.

"People first look at the length of the video and then the title," I said. He was going to use "Aaron Berlin for District Court Judge." But I suggested to use "Why Aaron?" It is shorter. It is concise. It begs for an answer.

Now having said that, sometimes you can post some of the most professional videos and get very little traction. Sometimes the worst videos can get traction. However, as my eighth-grade English teacher, Mr. Michael Rewald, said, "Even a blind pig finds an acorn every once in a while."

Mr. Rewald also said, "Everything is there when you become aware." Be aware of the fact that genuine pictures seem to get better traction than tailored photos. For instance, one Congressman had post after post about a bill he was trying to push through Congress. He was getting inconsequential traffic on these posts. Once he posted a picture of himself with his baby having a big giggle—he instantly received a lot of hits to his post. The Congressman had a genuine hearty smile and so did his baby.

It is okay to humanize yourself online. People appreciate those moments because they can relate. People also will re-post information when they are extremely angry about an issue. Either way, take notice of what works and what doesn't. Post based on these trends. In the end, the posts that strike high emotion will likely win the most views.

When to Post

When to post on social media is a fascinating question. Online engineers are still trying to fine-tune this component. Currently, there are three main social media accounts: Twitter, Facebook, and Instagram. According to Socialbakers, which did a study of over eleven thousand tweets, your ideal number of tweets per day should not be more than three. Once you pass three, engagement starts to dwindle. For

Facebook, you should post about every three days or so to keep viewers engaged. There is an exception, though. If you have over ten thousand viewers, you should post twice a day, according to an article by Forbes. Instagram is different. If you post fifteen times a day, it is fine as long as you post fifteen times a day every day. You must be consistent with Instagram to maximize your marketing efforts.

Do keep in mind, however, an ideal time to spread information is Tuesday morning. Now, does this mean you will always be able to post solely on Tuesday mornings? No. Situations come up and messages need to be relayed at all hours of the day. However, Tuesday through Thursday mornings are the best times. Sunday evenings can be a good time, too. The reason being that these are the most likely times people are looking for a little respite or distraction and will roam the internet. These are also the times they share posts.

You want others to share your messages, of course. Tuesday morning is the best time, however, because people are at work and have time to share it with other people throughout the entire week. It is a much better time than, say, 5:00 p.m. on a Monday night.

Get Others to Re-post

Who are your strongest supporters? Ask them to re-post your posts or to allow you to post on their pages. Then, rotate whose page you use. My sister, for example, was trying to garner support for twelve homeless cats and kittens to be vaccinated, sterilized, and adopted. In order to pay for the medical procedures, she needed to raise over $2,500. My sister decided to reach out to people by posting a "GoFundMe page" on various homeowners association Facebook pages. Throughout the process, she took photos about those helping and the cats being assisted. She then went back to the same Facebook pages with updates and the photos taken. In doing so, she kept folks informed and showed who was (proudly) helping and how enjoyable his or her experience was. Whether intentional or not, she kept the idea of donating money fresh on people's minds without having to annoyingly ask directly.

Another powerful post can be a testimonial. If you go above and beyond for a client, for example, the client is likely grateful. Ask if you can post a testimonial from that client. Sample testimonial: "I've had four knee surgeries and two physical therapists. I finally found a physical therapist who cares about my well-being instead of just documenting notes on my file." —Judy Hart.

A message like that is more powerful than you posting a message saying you are a company who cares. Plus, Judy is now someone the news can interview if need be. You can also ask Judy to re-post her testimonial. Most likely, she will say, yes. (Plus, Judy is an extra interview the news can use if they decide to do a story on your company. She will add dimension to the story.)

Someone else you should ask for help is the coordinator of an event. Let us say, for example, you are at an event and take a picture with the coordinator of the event. Ask the coordinator to share/tag you on social media and/or send the photo out via text message to others. The result? The leader of the group, who most likely has a following, will be promoting you. Best of all, it is a matter of one hand washing the other, because your followers will have exposure to the event. Good for the coordinator, good for you, and good for anyone interested in the information about the event.

No matter which approach you take, be sure to always write in first person. If you have someone else in charge of your social media accounts, make sure they know to write it as if you are the one typing it.

The importance of this can be found in the following cautionary example. One politician running for office posted something like, "I had a great time at our local high school today." The next day, his campaign manager posted on the same Facebook page something similar to "Great event for our candidate today." His social media page became confusing. The lesson here is—you or the communications director need to write in first person as though you are speaking to the voter or consumer on a personal level.

Most importantly, know that people will read about your information if it piques their interest, emotion, or relates to them. I saw one politician post something similar to this: "Here I am talking on the Senate floor in support of my bill about assessing mental health stability." Well, no kidding, you support your bill. It is, after all, your bill. Obviously, you want to see your agenda pass. How about posting something less about you and more about the people you are trying to help—more like a news headline. Perhaps you could post a statistic: "30% of college students suffer from depression. Grades suffer. This is why we must pass my bill."

Notice my headline above only has seventeen words? According to research by BuzzSumo, fifteen to eighteen words in your Facebook headline receives the most engagement. You can create a story within fifteen words to intrigue others to read more. For the most engaging headlines on Facebook, involve these three-word combinations:

- Will make you . . .
- This is why . . .
- Can you guess . . .

The worst phrases were:

- Control of your . . .
- Your own business . . .
- Work for you . . .

For Twitter, the three most engaging headlines were:

- This is what . . .
- For first time . . .
- Things to know . . .

So it appears folks on Twitter focus on the latest or the newest. While this research is very helpful, know what works for your audience. Know what sparks curiosity in their minds. The headline you use is just as important as the information you wish to relay because you are telling your followers why they should care.

"Only 20 Fortune 500 companies actually engage with their customers on Facebook, while 83% have a presence on Twitter."
—Brandwatch

Your Website

Your website needs to be similar, in that it needs to show facts and figures, statistics the media might use. It also needs to represent the people—the voter or consumer—just as the news does. In order to access the news easily, you should provide one section of your site with a press page.

Your press page should have in this order:

1. Photos
2. B-Roll
3. Statistics
4. Press Releases
5. Links to additional information
6. Calendar of events occurring with you or your company in the future that may affect the future headlines of the day

Most people make the mistake of only having press releases on their media page. By posting the information the press needs—photos and videos—you allow the press to actually cover your story, thus making you one step ahead of all your competitors who only post words in black-and-white. Finally, quickly thank the press for all they do at the end. This short gesture is one that I have never seen utilized, but one that will be appreciated.

When you share information on your website, remember why you are working for others either in public service or in business. In the end, your success would not be possible without those who supported you. Your website is one of the single best ways to specifically tailor your message with purposeful intention.

Politicians, especially, too often have websites that only talk about themselves. Make yours about the people. Did you pass a bill, for example, that helped others? Did you save money for your constituents? Did you make a product easier to use? Did you make it easier for your clients to access information? More importantly, did the media cover it? I'm sure you passed an amazing bill or made life easier for a client that no one will ever know about. After all, you have a thankless job. How then, do we get people to hear about your success? If you passed an amazing bill or saved money, it does not have to be forgotten. Let voters and consumers know about it through your website in a way that the news would cover the story.

Here are some ways to make your website focused on others:

1. First, create a section on your website that shows "How I Work for You."
2. Second, categorize the sections. Make sure the categories are labeled in a way to promote your position. For instance, don't create a category named "Agriculture." Instead, call it: "Fighting for Farmers." Other sections could be called: "Saving Dollars" or "Fighting for Safety."
3. In three to five sentences, write about your bill and its effect on others. I know you will want to write more. Refrain. Provide a link to more information instead. Folks will do their research if they are interested.
4. Include testimonials. Never forget the power of testimonials.

5. Create a video. (Again, remember what was noted before: if you are a member of Congress, *do not use video from C-SPAN*. Too boring.) Use video that humanizes your work or footage of you on the news. Let us say you recently increased the number of police patrolling a town. Find a person who was helped by an officer. Ask the victim to go on camera and tell their story. Then you say something about why you implemented the program. As a business person, if there is a client impacted by your product, ask the client to appear on camera. (If you use your phone to interview someone, remember to turn your phone horizontally so it reflects the horizontal shape of TVs.)

> "US adults spend an average of 1 hour, 16 minutes each day watching video on digital devices."
>
> —Brandwatch

Drive More Traffic to Your Site

When focusing on the content of your website, be unconventional. Do not just post information about your brand or your agenda. Post information that will benefits others. Pets and animals, for example, always stir emotion. Have you ever noticed how an action that protects a victimized pet always stirs positive emotions? I am not saying you should cash in on Bambi. However, if you are an animal lover who likes to rescue dogs and cats, like myself, let it be known.

A "Jobs Available" section can be another sub-menu for your website. Folks will go to certain search engines online to look for jobs; make your website one of them. When you speak to business owners, ask them if they are looking to hire quality people. If they are, ask the business owner if you can add the open position to your "Jobs Available" section. For a politician who always promotes the idea of creating jobs, this is especially a useful tool. Each time a new job is added to your website, post it on social media as well.

Once someone is hired because of your website, tell all the news stations about this new marriage of employer/boss. It is a win-win for all involved. The news stations can interview the person who got the job. When the news station wants a comment from you about it, tell them this story is about Joe who got the job and Bob who built the company from the bottom up. The stations will use your comment most likely. Be humble.

You might also draw attention to your website by putting a huge statistic on your main page. Did you save your district money? Did you increase your client's portfolio by 3 percent and another's by 4 percent? Add these numbers up and show the total in a big, bold way on the front page of your website. Put the number on a huge picture of a calculator and continue to update the number. (Just make sure the number is accurate.)

People will remember the image of the calculator. People will remember you are saving them money. They may not always remember the exact amount, but they will remember you are working toward saving money. Of course, this can be a sticky situation if you cut the costs of someone's program. When North Carolina's Governor Pat McCrory ran for re-election, he noted he had saved the state money. However, a lot of teachers were not happy with that statistic because his tax cuts had affected their salaries. In contrast, when a city councilman from Clemmons, North Carolina, ran for office, he noted how much money he had saved the city. He was able to do so by consolidating trash pickup, but the city was still just as clean. This worked for him and he won the most votes.

Perhaps you hold a lot of information sessions. Put dates in big and bold text on the first page of your website. Make it easy for folks to access important information.

Another page on your website that will entice news stations are ways in which you are giving back to the community. Local stations especially like to promote community events that invite goodwill. If you or your company have an annual fundraiser or give to a charity, create a "Giving Back" page. Again, find someone who is affected by your contributions. Putting a face with a story makes your kind act more memorable and inspirational—because a person's story is usually remembered by the common person.

If none of these ideas seem to pique your interest and you want to find the most up-to-date trends of what consumers/voters/viewers are fascinated by, go to Nielsen ratings. Nielsen studies facts and figures and posts the trends on a regular basis. For example, according to Nielsen ratings, approximately 84 million people watched the first presidential debate between Hillary Clinton and Donald Trump. If I were a politician or businessman, I would have tried to capture that interest on my website. I would post a cartoon of each candidate and say, "Hillary Clinton or Donald Trump? Email us who you think will win. If you are right, win a free prize." The same idea could apply to an Oscar ballot or a March Madness bracket.

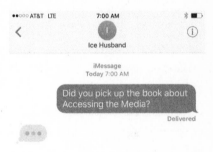

The Power of Text Messages

Think about President Obama's 2008 campaign. He utilized text message by sending out a message to millions to announce his pick for vice president, Joe Biden. He then used those millions of people to hold rallies and engage in an unconventional approach to raise a significant amount of money.

> "22 billion texts are sent every day worldwide, not including app-to-app messaging."
>
> —Text Request

While text messaging seemed unconventional back in 2008, it is extremely common and effective today. Even when raising money for your charity, it can be done through text messages or social media. Take the Red Cross, for example. When Haiti suffered a massive earthquake, the Red Cross stepped in to help collect donations. "A campaign using text messages to raise money for the Red Cross has tallied more than $21 million for relief efforts in Haiti," Doug Gross reported for CNN. "The electronic fundraiser, boosted in its early days by widespread posting on social-networking sites like Facebook and Twitter, has outstripped the organization's expectations and is showing no signs of letting up, an official said Monday." Gross noted that the $21 million smashed the previous Red Cross text-message campaign. The previous record was $4 million.

People won't see every update to your website, social media post, or email you send. However, people typically open up a text message. Text messages only take about five seconds to read. People appreciate the brevity of a text. Therefore, they are more likely to help you out when receiving a request through a text message rather than through email. Do be careful not to inundate people with messages. You must be very selective about what you send and how often. To avoid going in the spam folder, make sure you are consistent. Folks like to know when to anticipate your message.

Here is the bottom line, whether you are in business or in political office, posting information online or on your social media pages is a great way to send a message to the news indirectly. You can demonstrate the public's engagement in several ways:

1. a lot of attention on those pages,
2. a lot of people following you, or
3. a lot of comments being made.

If the public is intrigued, the news will be as well. After all, it is their job to know what information is creating a buzz. If the producers and reporters are doing their job, they should pick up what you put on your social media pages.

But don't wait for the news outlets to notice and come to you. Use the tactics outlined in this book in order to get the truth to the media. Keep this book handy and track what works for you and your team. Then email me, your media expert, at JillsMedia@gmail.com. Or you can go to my website, JillOsborn.com. If you strategically follow the tips throughout these pages, you will set yourself up for success when accessing the most powerful entity: the media.

Appendix A

Sample Press Releases

Here are guidelines for crafting press releases for a specific event. Adapt as needed for your own use.

Press Release #1

Below is an example of an event being held by a politician. Congresswoman Jane Doe is explaining to veterans some new options in health care. As her communications director, I want her to receive press coverage for the event. My job starts with some prep work:

1. First, I look at the headlines of the day for each news organization I want to contact. I get a feel for what stories are trending and see if our event relates to the headlines. If for example, there is no significant news relating to our event, but I know Veterans Day will be here next week, I can tie our story into the holiday nicely. I will make note of this in the email.

2. Second, I find out which reporter to call who might typically cover this event. I might reference the spreadsheet I created that tracks which reporters have been helpful in the past. I call each person directly because I, hopefully, have an individual cell phone number by now.

3. After a phone call is placed and the event is discussed with each reporter or news outlet, Press Release #1 is sent out. It

is never sent in a mass email. It is specifically sent to each reporter who expressed interest in the story.

4. Below is a sample press release. The story is presented to the news station as an event important to veterans. While Congresswoman Jane Doe's office set up the event, and she is the main speaker of the event, I am not promoting her. The event is about the veterans. I also talk about one veteran in particular to put a face with the story.

5. In the subject line of the email, I write: "Reporter's Name—Story Idea."

6. Finally, I will attach additional information, photos, and videos for the reporter's benefit and discretion.

Sample Press Release #1

"The Veterans Health Administration is the largest integrated health care system in the United States, providing care at 1,243 health care facilities, including 170 VA Medical Centers and 1,063 outpatient sites of care of varying complexity (VHA outpatient clinics), serving more than 9 million enrolled Veterans each year."—www.va.gov/health/

With Veterans Day approaching us next week, I thought this story might fit nicely in your lineup.

Who: Veterans of Foreign Wars (VFW). Richard Rice, past Post Commander, cooks a feast for his fellow comrades every Thursday at the VFW. However, he can't receive answers from the U.S. Department of Veterans Affairs (VA) about which hospital he needs to go to for a total knee replacement.

What: VA Health Information Session for Veterans

When: 5:00 Thursday

Where: VFW 100 Hampton Road, Clemmons

Why: With so many veterans qualifying for health care, there are bound to be some hiccups in the VA system.

Congressman Jane Doe provides some helpful answers on what to do and where veterans can go.

Contacts:

- Richard Rice, past Post Commander, Clemmons, VFW
  EMAIL: Rice@1234VFW.com
  CELL: (222) 555–1111
- Republican U.S. Congresswoman Jane Doe (NC-05)
  EMAIL: John Smith (Press Secretary) John@1234house.gov
  CELL: (555) 333–1111

Links for More Info:

www.VFW123.org, www.va.gov/health/, www.JaneDoe
/FightingforVeterans/.com

Attached is:

A video of Congresswoman Doe addressing the topic on CNN.

A two-minute video of the Congresswoman addressing the issue before Congress.

A photo of our veteran, Mr. Richard Rice.

A video of the Congresswoman speaking with Mr. Rice.

Press Release #2 for Television and Radio

The second press release is sent after a reporter does not attend the event. These press releases must be tailored specifically to each news medium. Here is a sample press release that can be used for television and radio. Again, the subject of the email will be: "Reporter Name—Story Idea." Remember, the sound in the video tells the story.

Sample Press Release #2

In case you need to add a story to your lineup . . . here is a breakdown from today's event:

[TAKE VO:] (NAT SOUNDS of meat sizzling in a pan and other various close-up scenes in the kitchen. All food being prepared by Mr. Rice.)

Everyone knows when Mr. Rice is at the VFW. Delicious aromas emanate from the kitchen where he is cooking. Every Thursday at 2:00, the man behind the apron prepares a feast for the men and women who have served our country. Mr. Rice works tirelessly and without complaint even though he needs a complete knee replacement. But, he cannot get answers from the VA. The pain continues, as does his cooking.

[TAKE SOT]

[CHYRON] Richard Rice Sr., past Post Commander, Clemmons, VFW

"I never miss a meal."

[TAKE VO] (Mr. Rice limping around the kitchen. Graphic of VA statistic. The Congresswoman being greeted by VFW.)

He also never hears a word back from the Department of Veterans Affair to answer the question of which hospital he can attend. It is no surprise. According to the VA's website, the Veterans Health Administration is America's largest integrated health-care system serving more than 9 million enrolled veterans each year. There is bound to be some errors.

[TAKE SOT] "It would be nice to get some answers."

[TAKE VO] (Henry Tree talking with other veterans.)

Henry Tree is also a veteran. He is frustrated and ready to cut through the red tape.

[TAKE SOT]

[CHYRON] Henry Tree, Veteran

"We need to know what is going on. We served our country overseas, but can't get help from our health-care system here at home."

[TAKE SOT]

[CHYRON] Rep. Jan Doe (NC-05)

"There are finally steps to better your health care. That's why I'm here. Because I care."

[TAKE VO] (The Congresswoman speaking at the podium. Wide shot of the crowd, etc.)

The VA is expanding the Veterans Choice Program which increases timely health care.

[TAKE GRAPHIC]

Even if veterans have VA health care, they are finally eligible to receive care in their community if: the veteran has not received care after more than 30 days, lives 40 miles away from a VA facility, or if traveling to a facility provides a constant burden.

Veterans can also call 1-866-606-8198 to see if they are eligible and to learn which doctors in their area may provide health care.

[TAKE SOT:] "I finally received an answer about where I can go to get help for my knee. I'm very happy to see her come to inform other veterans. Soon, I will be jumping around like I was nineteen again."

[TAKE SOT: REP.] "Our veterans served us and we need to serve them. Our office is always willing and eager to help."

[TAKE VO] (Mr. Rice serving food. Close-up of his knee. Folks laughing and eating with Mr. Rice.)

Despite any difficulties, like a good soldier, Mr. Rice continues to serve his fellow Americans.

Contacts:

- Richard Rice Sr., past Post Commander, Clemmons, VFW
  EMAIL: Rice@1234VFW.com
  CELL: (222) 555–1111
- Republican U.S. Congresswoman Jane Doe (NC-05)
  EMAIL: John Smith (Press Secretary) John@1234house.gov
  CELL: (555) 333–1111

- Henry Tree, Veteran
  EMAIL: Henry@1234gmail.com
  CELL: (123) 456–7890

If you would like to provide link to a website for more information on your website, veterans may go to www.JaneDoe/FightingforVeterans/.com.

Video and graphics are attached.

Please let me know if you need any additional information. I can make some calls and provide whatever is needed.

Press Release #2 for a Newspaper

Press Release #2 for newspapers will be different than it is for television and radio. More words and photos can be utilized here. Photos are the heart of the story, but your words also help paint the picture. Below is a sample:

Sample Press Release #2

In case you need to add a story to your lineup, here is a breakdown from today's event:

Sample Headlines: The Latest on Veteran Health Care, Veterans Get Answers, Expanding Health Care for Veterans

Richard Rice Sr., past Post Commander for the VFW in Clemmons, is at the Clemmons Post every Thursday at 2:00. Everyone knows when Mr. Rice is there because delicious aromas emanate from the kitchen.

"I never miss a meal," Mr. Rice says without looking up from the skillet. Mr. Rice has every reason to be at home. He needs a complete knee replacement and is in constant pain. However, he cannot get answers from the U.S. Department of Veterans Affairs (VA) about which hospital to receive care from for his knee.

It is no surprise Mr. Rice has heard nothing but crickets. According to the VA's website, "The Veterans Health Administration is the largest integrated health care system in the United States, providing care at 1,243 health care facilities, including 170 VA Medical Centers and 1,063 outpatient sites of care of varying complexity (VHA outpatient clinics), serving more than 9 million enrolled Veterans each year." With these kinds of numbers, there is bound to be some miscommunication.

Henry Tree is a veteran. He is frustrated and ready to cut through the red tape.

"We need to know what is going on," says Tree. "We served our country, yes, but we can't get help from our health-care system here at home."

Like Mr. Tree and Mr. Rice, many veterans came ready with questions for Congresswoman Jane Doe (NC-05). She was today's honored speaker at the VFW.

"There are finally steps to better your health care. That's why I'm here. Because I care," notes the Congresswoman.

In addition to answering questions, the Congresswoman supplied information on ways the VA are taking steps to provide better care for our service men and women. She noted that the VA is working to increase timely health care by expanding the Veterans Choice Program. The program will include information about the nearest VA medical facility. Veterans are finally eligible to receive care in their own community even if he or she has VA health care.

The eligibility requirements for community care are as follows: If the veteran has not received care after more than 30 days of his or her first attempt to get medical care, or if he or she lives 40 miles away from a VA facility, or if traveling to a facility provides an undue burden.

Veterans can also call 1-866-606-8198 to see if they are eligible and which doctors in their area may provide health care.

"Our veterans served us and we need to serve them. Our office is always willing and eager to help," volunteered Congresswoman Doe.

Mr. Rice acknowledges the information Congresswoman Doe provided is very helpful. "I finally received an answer about where to go to get help for my knee. I'm very happy to see her come to inform veterans. Soon, I hope to be jumping around like I was nineteen again."

For more information, please visit www.JaneDoe/Fightingfor Veterans/.com.

PHOTOS:
Pictured from left to right:
1. Richard Rice, Rep. Jane Doe, Steve Flow in red shirt
2. Jane Doe speaking at podium
3. Richard Rice serving food to Henry Tree
4. Henry Tree in blue suit, Jack Back in white shirt, Bill Thrill in VFW ball cap
5. Jane Doe talking to Bill Thrill

CONTACTS:
- Richard Rice Sr., past Post Commander, Clemmons, VFW
  EMAIL: Rice@1234VFW.com
  CELL: (222) 555–1111
- Republican U.S. Congresswoman Jane Doe (NC-05)
  EMAIL: John Smith (Press Secretary) John@1234house.gov
  CELL: (555) 333–1111
- Henry Tree, Veteran
  EMAIL: Henry@1234gmail.com
  CELL: (123) 456–7890
- Jack Back, Veteran
  EMAIL: Jack@1234gmail.com
  CELL: (123) 456–7890

- Bill Thrill, Veteran
  EMAIL: Bill@1234gmail.com
  CELL: (123) 456–7890

Also attached is a two-minute video of how Congresswoman Jane Doe fights for veterans in Congress.

Please let me know if you need any additional information. I can make some calls and provide whatever is needed.

Appendix B

Quiz: Do You Get the Media?

Let's test your media expertise. You can take this quiz before you read the book and afterward to test your knowledge and compare the results. In addition to passing the quiz with higher success rates after reading this book, you may observe how you watch the news differently. You may start to notice how and why each story is covered as opposed to simply paying attention to the facts presented to you. Either way, see if you need improvement or if you have already improved your knowledge when it comes to accessing the media.

Quiz: Do you get the media?

1. Should a TV newsroom and weekly newspaper receive a news release on the same day about the same event? Yes or No

2. If the press does not show up to your event, is there a chance they will cover it in the news? Yes or No

3. In a television news report, does the video have more impact on the story than the sound in the story? Yes or No

4. Is an MOS known as a Man on the Street interview? Yes or No

5. If you need to get out important information, should you send out a mass press release?   Yes or No

6. Do you leak information on social media before sending out a press release?   Yes or No

7. Do you provide videos in your press release?   Yes or No

8. Is B-Roll a news term for an exclusive interview?   Yes or No

9. Do you need to provide statistics in every single press release?   Yes or No

10. If you have three events for the press to cover, is it okay to send out more than one press release on the same day?   Yes or No

11. Is it impossible to find a booking producer by googling "Booking Producer?"   Yes or No

12. Do you call reporters to give them news tips?   Yes or No

13. Does a reporter typically wear high heels?   Yes or No

14. Is it important to which reporters in your area cover the business beat?   Yes or No

15. Should you ever give the reporter your typed notes after a debate or public speech?   Yes or No

Tally your score.

1. Yes: 0 points No: 1 point
   TV news should receive a press release the day of the event.

2. Yes: 1 point No: 0 points
   As long as you provide the photos or video, there is a chance your story will still be covered depending on the news of the day.

3. Yes: 0 points No: 1 point
   No, sound should tell the story for TV and radio. Video helps, but the sounds catch the emotion. Imagine a team winning a game at the end of the buzzer. It is much more

impactful to hear the sound of the buzzer, see the shot go in, and hear the crowd roar, as opposed to looking at the clock count down and looking at the shot.

4. Yes: 1 point No: 0 points
A Man on the Street (MOS) puts a face with the story, therefore creating a more emotional reaction from the viewer, helping them remember the story.

5. Yes: 0 points No: 1 point
No one likes a mass press release.

6. Yes: 1 point No: 0 points
Your social media pages should be a source of information for the news.

7. Yes: 1 point No: 0 points
The right kind of video will get your foot in the door.

8. Yes: 0 points No: 1 point
B-Roll is extra video of the event.

9. Yes: 1 point No: 0 points
Absolutely. Statistics make stories interesting and relatable.

10. Yes: 0 points No: 1 point
Be strategic about what you send out and to whom. Do not inundate someone's email inbox.

11. Yes: 0 points No: 1 point
This is false. If you google booking producer, a whole slew of "Booking Producer," is provided, as well as who they work for, and what social media page they utilize the most. (If you cannot find their contact information online, contact them through their most-utilized social media outlet.)

12. Yes: 1 point No: 0 points
You will create rapport with reporters by giving them tips.

13. Yes: 0 points No: 1 point
Reporters are out in the field at the remote lake covering the missing persons story and going live at 5:00 while crews continue their search. Hardly high heel terrain. Reporters

wear shoes with a spare pair of rain boots in the trunk. Anchors wear heels because they are steadily in studio.

14. Yes: 1 point No: 0 points

    You need to know who to call when marketing your story. Specific reporters typically cover specific news stories, also known as beats. You must know who covers the beat in which your story would appear.

15. Yes: 1 point No: 0 points

    Sure. Handing over notes right after an event, or telling a reporter you will send your answers via email as soon as you get home, makes the job easier for the reporter. It is also better for you. You will be more likely to be quoted if the reporter has your notes at their discretion—and you won't have to worry about being misquoted.

Media Quiz Scorecard

0–5 points: News Novice You should refer to this book and try to pay attention to the news more often to see which medium covers which stories. This book will continue to help you understand the how and why of news coverage.

6–10 points: Informed Watcher You likely stay tuned to the news stories of the day. You have an idea of what you are doing. This book will help you continue to understand why your ideas have or have not been working in the past. It will provide a good reference for you in the future.

11–15 points: Eye for the News Great work. You have likely been involved in the news on some level, whether you have worked for the news or been the story. Keep up the good work, and as the book says, keep tracking what works for you and what does not.

Feel free to email me about your success: JillsMedia@gmail.com.

Source Notes

Chapter 1: Why You Need the Press

Kruger explains the psychology . . .
Stephanie Pappas, "Oscar Psychology: Why Celebrities Fascinate Us,"
    last modified February 24, 2012, https://www.livescience
    .com/18649-oscar-psychology-celebrity-worship.html

For Chinese reporters, it is even worse.
Niemen Foundation, "The State of Journalism in China," last
    modified November 12, 2016, http://nieman.harvard.edu/books
    /the-state-of-journalism-in-china/

In Mexico, a journalist was gunned down . . .
Associated Press, "Journalist Javier Valdez shot to death in Mexico
    drug state," last modified May 16, 2017, http://www.foxnews.com
    /world/2017/05/16/journalist-javier-valdez-shot-to-death-in-mexico-
    drug-state.html

In 2006, the journalist Anna Politkovskaya was murdered . . .
Michael Specter, "Kremlin, Inc.: Why are Vladimir Putin's opponents
    dying?" last modified January 29, 2007, http://www.newyorker
    .com/magazine/2007/01/29/kremlin-inc

However, the CPJ notes the top three most censored countries are . . .
Committee to Protect Journalists, "10 Most Censored Countries,"
accessed January 19, 2018, https://cpj.org/2015/04/10-most-
censored-countries.php
However, voters always remembered "email scandal" . . .
Jason Le Miere, "Did the Media Help Donald Trump Win? $5
Billion in Free Advertising Given to President-Elect," last modified
November 9, 2016, http://www.ibtimes.com/did-media-help-
donald-trump-win-5-billion-free-advertising-given-president-
elect-2444115

Every two years the American politics industry fills the airwaves . . .
Charles Krauthammer, "Charles Krauthammer quotes," accessed
January 19, 2018, https://www.brainyquote.com/quotes/charles
_krauthammer_409487

$1.2 Billion. The amount of . . .
Bob Fredericks, "Hillary Clinton's losing campaign cost a record $1.2
B," last modified December 9, 2016, https://nypost.com/2016/12/09
/hillary-clintons-losing-campaign-cost-a-record-1-2b/

$5 Billion . . .
Jason Le Miere, "Did the Media Help Donald Trump Win? $5
Billion in Free Advertising Given to President-Elect," last modified
November 9, 2016, http://www.ibtimes.com/did-media-help-
donald-trump-win-5-billion-free-advertising-given-president-
elect-2444115

. . . Councilmen buy stake in Chronicle.
Wesley Young, "Councilmen buy stake in *Chronicle*," last modified
March, 29, 2017, http://www.journalnow.com/news/local/two-
on-winston-salem-city-council-part-of-group-buying/article_
a82b6b5a-e1df-562b-90f1-51a32208cbac.html

Fake media has started to make its presence . . .

Ben Westcott, "Duped by fake news story, Pakistani minister
    threatens nuclear war with Israel," last modified December 26,
    2016, http://www.cnn.com/2016/12/26/middleeast/israel-pakistan-
    fake-news-nuclear/index.html

In April 2017, Germany decided to take a stance . . .

Emma Thomasson, "German cabinet agrees to fine social media over
    hate speech," last modified April 5, 2017, http://www.reuters.com
    /article/us-germany-hatecrime-idUSKBN1771FC

Fake news does influence your thought process . . .

Dr. Mehmet Oz, "Dr. Oz: EEG Brain Scans Reveal Fake News
    Threatens Your Health," last modified February 22, 2017, http://
    observer.com/2017/02/dr-mehmet-oz-fake-news-bad-for-health/

. . . when Apple is in the news.

Dino Grandoni, "Apple's Marketing Secret: Hold Off On The Ads,
    Ride The Hype," last modified September 19, 2012, http://www.
    huffingtonpost.com/2012/08/06/apple-marketing-secret-phil-
    schiller_n_1749313.html

According to the report, advertisers will have spent . . .

Brandon Katz, "Digital Ad Spending Will Surpass TV Spending for
    the First Time in US History," last modified September 14, 2016,
    https://www.forbes.com/sites/brandonkatz/2016/09/14/digital-
    ad-spending-will-surpass-tv-spending-for-the-first-time-in-u-s-
    history/#53671ff74207

Chapter 2: Getting Press Coverage: A Behind-the-Scenes Look

Utilize every media outlet out there.

Ashley Papa, email message to author, October 12, 2016

Even if Americans don't trust the government . . .

John Sides, "Americans don't trust government. But they still want government to do a lot," last modified November 23, 2015, https://www.washingtonpost.com/news/monkey-cage/wp/2015/11/23/americans-dont-trust-government-but-they-still-want-government-to-do-a-lot/?utm_term=.da389f40e272

Put a Face on the Story . . .

Al Tompkins, *Aim for the Heart* (Thousand Oaks, California: CQ Press College, 2017)

For proof, look at any winner . . .

Dave Phillipps, "Disposable: Surge in discharges includes wounded soldiers," last modified May 19, 2013, http://cdn.csgazette.biz/soldiers/day1.html

Chapter 3: Three Points of Contact

. . if fighting for equal pay and affordable childcare . . .

Katie Reilly, "Read President Obama and Hillary Clinton's Remarks From Their First Joint Rally," last modified July 5, 2016, http://time.com/4394191/barack-obama-hillary-clinton-rally-transcript/

Clinton's appearance came a day after her mother's . . .

Wesley Young, "Chelsea Clinton at Wake Forest: College is a women's issue," last modified September 13, 2016, http://www.journalnow.com/news/local/chelsea-clinton-at-wake-forest-college-is-a-women-s/article_e9088cef-6bf1-567e-982f-04aa0465f8c4.html

I would rather excel . . .

Alexander the Great, "Alexander the Great Quote on Dominion," accessed January 19, 2018, https://allauthor.com/quotes/133473/

Success leaves clues.

Team Tony, "The Key to Success? Model the Best," accessed January

20, 2018, https://www.tonyrobbins.com/stories/the-key-to-success-model-the-best/

As a news organization, we get hundreds of emails . . .
Jeff Gravley, email to author, October 12, 2016

Chapter 4: The Inner Workings of a Newsroom
Be sincere; be brief; be seated.
Franklin D. Roosevelt, "Quotes by Franklin D. Roosevelt," accessed
    January 19, 2018, https://www.brainyquote.com/quotes/quotes/f/
    franklind164074.html

Ask not what your country can do for you . . .
Jack Kennedy, "Ask not what your country can do for you . . ."
    accessed January 21, 2018, https://www.jfklibrary.org/Education/
    Teachers/Curricular-Resources/Elementary-School-Curricular-
    Materials/Ask-Not.aspx

Chapter 5: First Point of Contact: Before the Event
People like people who . . .
Jack Schafer, "Six Tips to Get Higher Tips: Techniques that
    Predispose Customers to Leave Higher Tips," last modified July
    18, 2012, https://www.psychologytoday.com/blog/let-their-words-
    do-the-talking/201207/six-tips-get-higher-tips

A drop of honey . . .
Abraham Lincoln, "Abraham Lincoln > Quotes > Quotable
    Quotes," accessed January 19, 2018, https://www.goodreads.com/
    quotes/669287-a-drop-of-honey-gathers-more-flies-than-a-gallon

Famous Eagle Scouts . . .
Joseph Bork et al., "Eagle Scout Information," accessed January 19, 2018, http://www.usscouts.org/eagle/bsfamous.asp

The total percentage . . .
Boy Scout Statistics, "Boy Scout Statistics," accessed January 19, 2018, http://www.statisticbrain.com/boy-scout-statistics/

As Mark Twain once said . . .
Mark Twain, "Mark Twain > Quotes > Quotable Quotes," accessed January 19, 2018, https://www.goodreads.com/quotes/7282642-an-honest-man-in-politics-shines-more-there-than-he

Jim Williams is an award-winning journalist . . .
Jim Williams, email to author, October 21, 2016

Chapter 6: Timing: When to Contact Each News Outlet

Do what you can . . .
Theodore Roosevelt, "Theodore Roosevelt Quotes," accessed January 19, 2018, https://www.brainyquote.com/quotes/quotes/t/theodorero100965.html

Chapter 7: Going Live in Studio

Remember what Winston Churchill said . . .
Winston Churchill, "Winston Churchill > Quotes > Quotable Quotes," accessed January 19, 2018, https://www.goodreads.com/quotes/218-a-politician-needs-the-ability-to-foretell-what-is-going

Chapter 8: Second Point of Contact: Greet the Reporter

Mahatma Gandhi had a different opinion . . .

Mahatma Gandhi, "Mahatma Gandhi Quotes," accessed January 19, 2018, https://www.brainyquote.com/quotes/quotes/m/mahatmagan105881.html

I've learned that . . .
Maya Angelou, "Maya Angelou > Quotes," accessed January 19, 2018, http://www.goodreads.com/author/quotes/3503.Maya_Angelou

If you treat people right . . .
Franklin D. Roosevelt, "Franklin D. Roosevelt > Quotes > Quotable Quotes," accessed January 19, 2018, https://www.goodreads.com/quotes/30644-if-you-treat-people-right-they-will-treat-you-right

Chapter 9: Third Point of Contact: You Are the Reporter

The newspaper sold over 1.15 million copies . . .
Stephan Benzkofer, "The JFK assassination: 50 years later," last modified November 10, 2013, http://articles.chicagotribune.com/2013-11-10/site/ct-per-flash-jfk-1110-20131110_1_jfk-assassination-chicago-board-50-years

Chapter 10: The Newspaper

It's amazing the amount of news . . .
Jerry Seinfeld, "Quotes by Jerry Seinfeld," accessed January 19, 2018, https://www.brainyquote.com/quotes/quotes/j/jerryseinf100233.html

Observe the list of presidential candidates . . .
Taylor Adams et al., "New York Times Endorsements through the Ages: A collection of The Times's endorsements for the presidency, from Abraham Lincoln in 1860 through the editorial board's choice of Hillary Clinton in 2016," last modified September 23, 2016, https://www.nytimes.com/interactive/2016/09/23/opinion/presidential-endorsement-timeline.html?_r=1

One guiding factor for editors . . .
Guy Bergstorm, "Understanding the News Cycle at a Newspaper:
The Time of Day-And Day of the Week-Matters," last modified
June 11, 2017, https://www.thebalance.com/understanding-the-
news-cycle-2295933

As an example, only 24 percent . . .
Jim Moore, "Do American Trust the Media?" last modified August
15, 2017, https://www.huffingtonpost.com/entry/do-americans-
trust-the-media_us_598cdfdde4b0ed1f464c09af

Chapter 11: How to Record for TV and Radio
FOX Sports actually encouraged . . .
Nascar.com, "FOX SPORTS REVEALS SPECIAL DAYTONA
PROGRAMMING," last modified January 19, 2016, http://
www.nascar.com/en_us/news-media/articles/2016/1/19/fox-sports-
announces-daytona-500-programming-2016.html

When Gretchen Carlson was suing . . .
Oriana Schwindt, "Gretchen Carlson Offers Support for Victims of
Sexual Harassment With Twitter Video," last modified July 19,
2016, http://variety.com/2016/tv/news/gretchen-carlson-twitter-
video-message-fox-news-roger-ailes-1201817635/

One study sponsored by Xerox . . .
Xerox, "20 Ways to Share the Color Knowledge," accessed January
19, 2018, http://www.office.xerox.com/latest/COLFS-02UA.PDF

Chapter 12: Social Media
eMarketer projects that mobile ad spending . . .
Brandon Katz, "Digital Ad Spending Will Surpass TV Spending
For The First Time in U.S. History," last modified September

14, 2016, https://www.forbes.com/sites/brandonkatz/2016/09/14/
digital-ad-spending-will-surpass-tv-spending-for-the-first-time-in-
u-s-history/#46866d9d4207

Social media statistics . . .
Kit Smith, "Marketing: 96 Amazing Social Media Statistics and
Facts," last modified March 7, 2016, https://www.brandwatch.
com/blog/96-amazing-social-media-statistics-and-facts-for-2016/

According to a new study by computer scientists . . .
Caitlin Dewey, "6 in 10 of you will share this link without reading
it, a new, depressing study," last modified June 16, 2016, https://
www.washingtonpost.com/news/the-intersect/wp/2016/06/16/six-
in-10-of-you-will-share-this-link-without-reading-it-according-to-a-
new-and-depressing-study/?utm_term=.7acd348a97ef

By clicking on a 'thumbs up' or 'thumbs down' icon . . .
Mary Cate Cary, "5 Ways New Media Are Changing Politics," last
modified February 4, 2010, https://www.usnews.com/opinion/
articles/2010/02/04/5-ways-new-media-are-changing-politics

A majority of U.S. adults . . .
Jeffrey Gottfried et al., "News Use Across Social Media Platforms
2016," last modified May 26, 2016, http://www.journalism.
org/2016/05/26/news-use-across-social-media-platforms-2016/

Even a blind pig finds an acorn . . .
Mr. Michael Rewald, in conversation with author, August 2016

According to Socialbakers, which did a study . . .
Socialbakers, "Tweeting too Much? Find Out the Ideal Tweet
Frequency for Brands," accessed January 20, 2018, https://www.
socialbakers.com/blog/1847-tweeting-too-much-find-out-the-ideal-
tweet-frequency-for-brands

If you have over ten thousand viewers . . .
Neil Patel, "How Frequently You Should Post on Social Media According to the Pros," last modified September 12, 2016, https://www.forbes.com/sites/neilpatel/2016/09/12/how-frequently-you-should-post-on-social-media-according-to-the-pros/#57a72af8240f

According to research by BuzzSumo . . .
Steve Rayson, "We Analyzed 100 Million Headlines. Here's What We Learned (New Research)," last modified June 26, 2017, http://buzzsumo.com/blog/most-shared-headlines-study/

Only 20 Fortune 500 companies . . .
Kit Smith, "Marketing: 105 Amazing Social Media Statistics and Facts," last modified November 18, 2017, https://www.brandwatch.com/blog/96-amazing-social-media-statistics-and-facts-for-2016/

US adults spend an average . . .
Kit Smith, "Marketing: 105 Amazing Social Media Statistics and Facts," last modified November 18, 2017, https://www.brandwatch.com/blog/96-amazing-social-media-statistics-and-facts-for-2016/

Nielsen studies facts and figures . . .
Nielsen Ratings, "FIRST PRESIDENTIAL DEBATE OF 2016 DRAWS 84 MILLION VIEWERS," last modified September 27, 2016, http://www.nielsen.com/us/en/insights/news/2016/first-presidential-debate-of-2016-draws-84-million-viewers.html

22 billion texts . . .
Kenneth Burke, "73 Texting Statistics That Answer All Your Questions," last modified 2017, https://www.textrequest.com/blog/texting-statistics-answer-questions/

Take the Red Cross, for example.
Doug Gross, "Red Cross text donations pass $21 million," last
    modified January 18, 2010, http://www.cnn.com/2010/
    TECH/01/18/redcross.texts/index.htmlred

Appendix A: Sample Press Releases
The Veterans Health Administration . . .
Veterans Health Administration, "About VHA," accessed January 20,
    2018, https://www.va.gov/health/aboutVHA.asp

About the Author

Jill Osborn comes with a full-court press. She has experience in the national news and federal government, and she is a co-owner of a successful business.

Osborn is an award-winning columnist and political correspondent. She worked in a congressional office on Capitol Hill and for a top DC lobbying firm and went on to be a contributor at FOX News. Jill lives with her husband and children in North Carolina.